KNOWING HÎM

The indictment that started it all for me:

Job 36:26 "Behold God is great, and <u>we know Him not</u>, neither can the number of His years be searched out."

Edwin D. Button

BAPTIST TRAINING CENTER PUBLICATIONS
WINTER HAVEN, FLORIDA

Copyright © 2023 Edwin D. Button
All rights reserved. This book or any portion thereof may not be reproduced, distributed, or transmitted in any form or by any means, including photocopying, recording, or other electronic or mechanical methods, without the express written permission of the publisher or copyright holder except for the use of brief quotations as allowed by section 107 of the United States copyright law.

First Edition, 2023

Printed in the United States of America by:

A Ministry of:
Westwood Missionary Baptist Church
Winter Haven, FL
www.baptisttrainingcenter.org

Edwin D. Button, 1956 -
    Knowing Him / Button, Edwin D.
    1. Nonfiction > Religion > Christian Life > Spiritual Growth
    2. Nonfiction > Religion > Christian Life > Personal Growth
ISBN 13: 978-1-947598-23-2
ISBN 10: 1-947598-23-6

There is no greater pursuit in life than the pursuit of knowing God. Within the heart of every human is a need to intimately know the Creator and to walk with Him. In my experience in life, I have never met anyone with a greater passion for knowing and walking with the Lord than Ed Button. I have always been amazed at the thought of the apostle Paul, who knew the Lord intimately, saying, "That I may know him." Knowing Ed Button for 20 years, I am equally amazed that he still desires to know the Lord more as I have been an eye witness to his deep, abiding relationship with God. Within the pages of this book, you will find practical ways in which you can know the Lord better. Some avenues that are outlined in this book are enjoyable, while others may make you uncomfortable. However, if you will read these pages with a prayerful heart that desires to know the Lord in a deeper and more intimate way, you will find help for your journey of "Knowing Him."

Eric Sutton
President, American Baptist Association
Pastor, New Home Baptist Church
Wetumpka, Alabama

Contents

Acknowledgments 7
Introduction 9
1. Knowing Him in His Pardon 11
2. Knowing Him in His Person 19
3. Knowing Him in His Peace 25
4. Knowing Him in the Pages 33
5. Knowing Him in His Passion 41
6. Knowing Him in His Punishment 49
7. Knowing Him in His Purity 59
8. Knowing Him in His Power 67
9. Knowing Him in His Pain 75
10. Knowing Him in His Praises 83
11. Knowing Him in Prayer 89
12. Knowing Him in His Promises 97

Acknowledgments

Although this work has been on my heart for some time, it could never have come to fruition without the incredible support from my wife, church family, close network of friends and of course the aid of the Holy Spirit of God. I pause to thank God for hand-picking my Godly parents, my siblings, my Sunday School teachers, and the great men of God that invested in me, pouring their passion and ministry expertise into me. I am blessed to have many colleagues in the ministry that encourage and prop me up in prayer. I do not take that for granted. I also want to thank one of my grandchildren, Takoda Button, for his graphic artwork on the book cover.

More than once I have questioned God's direction only to discover that He knew the way and the outcome and was working all things for my good. On the night before my earthly father died, I was walking the country road where I live and asking God why my dad was dying; I started singing familiar songs and without any strategy I started singing "Trust and Obey;" being happy in Jesus really is dependent on it. I needed that reminder; His ways are higher than my ways (Isaiah 55:8-9).

Introduction

I have enjoyed the privilege of pastoring two of the Lord's churches: the first in Jacksonville and the second in a rural setting just outside Webster, both in Florida. Both were great experiences for me more than for them but blessed, nonetheless. The second great church became my family and the biggest part of my social circle. As I invested in them, so did they in me and my blood family. One of the greatest compliments I ever received came from a dear friend during a testimony he shared with a group of Christian men. He stated that there were three pastors in his life for which he would forever be grateful. The first introduced him to Jesus as his personal savior, the second taught him to stand on the truth of the Bible, and the third (I am thinking that this one was me) taught him "to know the Lord". Somewhere near the thirty-year mark as pastor of Gant Lake Baptist Church, I began focusing on "Knowing Him". If I had only one message left in me, only one more time that I would stand behind the sacred desk, then my message would be "**Know Him.**"

In 1980 while pastoring in Jacksonville I met a man named Carl. I was visiting prospects that lived off of Beach Boulevard. We were both walking the sidewalk when this well-dressed man introduced himself. After a few pleasantries were exchanged I found that he too was a preacher, and he was just out door-knocking for the Lord. Shortly we exchanged business cards and were on our way. Later when I wanted to reflect on this encounter, I took a closer look at his business card which read:

> *My name is Carl, it was a pleasure to meet you today. If our meeting today is soon forgotten, there is very little lost. But if I have introduced you to Jesus and that meeting is forgotten, then my friend, everything is lost.*

About a decade later I discovered two books written by the same author: the first was "The Pursuit of God" and the second was "The Knowledge of the Holy". Although he may not have been my "go to" doctrinal guide, these two books identified a short coming and/or a weakness in my Christian walk. These nudges were strategic to awaken a passion in me to really, deeply, and intimately "know Him".

This pursuit on which I embarked was a desire of many Bible characters. They would acknowledge their lacking and ignorance of Him and many of the challenges they faced on their journey. A journey that I felt compelled to make. There is nothing about this book intended to suggest that I finally made it. The truth is that although God and the knowledge of God is not an elusive or aloof pursuit, my journey has only convinced me of how little I knew when I began my journey. Like the Apostle Paul, I would like to be found still pressing toward the mark. In January of 2010 in my daily through the Bible readings, I decided to look for and highlight all the passages in the Bible that dealt with "knowing Him." By the end of that year my daily reading Bible was highlighted everywhere. God has invited us to "know Him." He has no fear of us knowing too much; that some-how we will discover the dark secrets. God has no skeletons in His closet. The opposite is true, the more that we know Him means the more that we love Him. My prayer is that you will accept the challenge to "know Him" not just about Him (although that is a good place to start) not just a fact-finding mission; but a life altering intimate knowledge of God and His Christ.

Chapter One

KNOWING HIM IN HIS PARDON

> "Let the wicked forsake his way, and the unrighteous man his thoughts: and let him return unto the LORD, and He will have mercy upon him; and to our God, for He will abundantly pardon." Isaiah 55:7
>
> "If the Son therefore shall make you free, ye shall be free indeed." John 8:36

Fundamental and foundational to all knowledge of the LORD is knowing Him as Saviour. It seems only right that this journey like every journey should begin with the first step. The knowledge of Christ is not accidental or haphazardly acquired. It is a pursuit that demands an orderly approach. Man was created in the image or likeness of God but through an act of rebellion and wanton disobedience man fell from his innocence and lost his home and his fellowship with a holy God. That which was lost in the garden of Eden, God has made a way to restore through the offering of His Son Jesus as a spotless sacrifice for our sin. By faith in the work of Christ at Calvary to pay your sin debt and by your confession of sin, that fellowship will be restored. This work of God's grace is known by many terms: justification, salvation, born again, redeemed, etc. However, this is not the finish line but the start gate. This "Knowing Him" journey is a process that is affected by time, effort, and passion but it begins with the Pardon from the Lord.

Pardon as defined by Webster is: 1) to absolve from the consequences of a fault or crime; 2) to allow (an offense) to pass without punishment: FORGIVE. Pardon does not eliminate one's guilt but releases one from the prosecution for the crime. In the eyes of the law, you are blameless, a diplomat without condemnation. In America we see pardon given at the end of a presidential term for presumed innocent people, for political prisoners, for genuinely repentant folk or for campaign contributors. Some have maintained their innocence others have confessed their guilt, but both are exonerated and restored to their prior liberty. That is exactly what happens to a person that confesses their sin to God and puts faith in the payment for sin that Christ paid with His own life at Calvary. Relationship and liberty are restored to the prior status (before sin).

I consider myself to have been quite fortunate in my up bringing; I was raised in a Christian home and was routinely in church. In fact, I was in church nine months before I was born. Going to the house of God has never been an option for me, that is all I know. As a salute to my parents I can say, "Thank you for giving me a head start in my quest to know the Lord." At an early age I remember the puzzling language of the elders and wondering if I would ever be trusted with the decoder. Often it was during prayers that I would scratch my head. I heard phrases like: "Father guard his lips as he stands behind the sacred desk" or "Father, hide him behind the cross" or one of my favorites, "until all shall know thee in the free pardon of sin." I was confused. To me as a young boy it sounded like, "freepardonasin." I didn't know that it was more than one word and frankly as fast as they said it, I wasn't entirely sure that it was more than one syllable. Well, I grew up and started using many of those same lines myself even if I didn't completely comprehend them. Though much older now I have never come to understand why God would allow His Son, Jesus, to die the cruel, vicious, and vicarious death of the cross of Calvary to buy my pardon. Thankfully, I don't have to understand it to benefit from or enjoy it. I really don't understand television or microwave ovens, but I enjoy them almost every day.

Of the many paradox' in scripture, two that are very precious to me are found in Paul's second letter to the church in Corinth. The first is in chapter five and verse twenty-one. "For He hath made Him to be sin for us, who knew no sin; that we might be made the righteousness of God in Him." And the second is found in chapter eight and verse nine. "For we know the grace of our Lord Jesus Christ, that, though He was rich, yet for your sakes he became poor, that ye through His poverty might be rich." These two great passages help me to understand the "what" of my pardon even if it doesn't help me with the "why" of my pardon. The Apostle Paul, a man trained in law, uses logic and parallelism to argue or defend his case for justification or reconciliation. In the Old Testament, the word "pardon" is used sixteen times. And although the word pardon is not used in the New Testament there are many synonym words used like: justified, reconciled, forgiven, born-again, atoned, redeemed and free indeed. (See Romans 3:19-26, Romans 5:1-10, John 3:7, John 8:36, Galatians 3:13, Ephesians 4:32 & Colossians 2:13) Paul's compelling arguments for pardon appear in almost every letter God inspired him to write but it is the subject of his writing to the saints in Rome. Paul begins by declaring the universal guilt of all men from every era and from every people group, ethnicity, culture, or social status. By the time one navigates through the book of Romans and arrives at chapter eight he will find that there is a universal cure for a universal problem. Paul addresses three truths associated with our pardon.

The Legality of This Pardon

Article II and section 2 of the Constitution of the United States of America affords the President of the United States the power to grant reprieves and pardons for certain offenses against the United States. This power has been exercised many times and refused relatively few times; it is clear however that proper conditions must be met. Only the president and only in matters under his authority (federal offenses) can pardons be issued and/or enforced. It would be laughable for me to think that I could draft up some legal document and present it to the warden at the federal prison near my home and expect my friends or family to be set free. I don't have that right or power. A pardon is an official action recognized by our justice system if it has been signed by or enacted by the appropriate authority. Regarding the guilty verdict that hangs over all of our heads, there is only one who has the power to dismiss the charges or provide a pardon and that is Jesus the Son of God. According to John 5:22-27 God the Father has granted all authority in judgment over to His Son. Since sin is an infraction against God and His holy standard, it stands to reason that God, or the agent of His choosing would be the only legal resource for or avenue of pardon. The depths of the crime do not bear any impact on the validity of the pardon. It is sometimes difficult for me to see the severity of my own crimes/sins but easy to see the sins of others. I doubt my ability to be an impartial judge. Many years ago, I failed miserably as an umpire by calling my son out at home plate when I knew he was safe; but, in a bang bang play and with the game on the line I called him out in order to silence the critics. To save face with the visiting team and their coaching staff, I lost credibility with my son. God is holy and righteous in all matters of judgment. I am reminded that it is difficult to examine the mote in my brother's eye while a beam is in my own eye. (Matthew 7:1-5) I tend to consider my crimes as petty, and others sins as grievous. To God, all sin disqualifies us for Heaven and must be paid for by death. That is what He told Adam in the garden. That is what He told Moses on Mt. Nebo. But thanks be to God that pardon is available in Christ who paid that debt with His own blood. There is an old hymn that I love, "To God Be the Glory"; but I am especially drawn to the second verse:

> "Oh, perfect redemption, the purchase of blood, To every believer the promise of God; The vilest offender who truly believes, That moment from Jesus a pardon receives. Praise the Lord praise the Lord, Let the earth hear His voice; Praise the Lord, praise the Lord, Let the people rejoice; Oh, come to the Father, through Jesus the Son, And give Him the glory; great things He hath done."

In Romans 8:33 & 34 Paul provided for us the credentials that qualify Jesus to pardon. He said, "Who shall lay any thing to the charge of God's elect? It is God that justifieth. Who is he that condemneth? It is Christ that died, yea rather, that is risen again, who is even at the right hand of God, who also maketh intercession for us." If you still doubt the right or power of Jesus to forgive sin, then you are in the company of the pretentious scribes of Jesus' day. They accused the Lord of blasphemy for His kind act of forgiveness. (Matthew 9:1-8) It is clear that the main reason for the miracles of Christ' ministry was to confirm His power to forgive sin.

The Liberty of This Pardon

With a pardon comes the reinstatement of liberties lost. It must have been precious to Adam and Eve that the Lord God promised redemption through the seed of woman (Genesis 3:15). A restoration of what had been lost as a result of sin. Sin has consequences and we must live with those consequences today; but in light of the liberty available to us in Christ. A pardoned criminal may be loosed back into society but hardly without consequences. Trust has been violated, homes destroyed, financial hardship created, neighborhoods betrayed, and a nation injured. Not everyone will embrace this freedom you have been given. Nonetheless, it is yours to enjoy and pursue and with the passing of time society may open their arms to embrace you again. Who knows? It might be forgotten entirely since the record has been expunged. There are levels or degrees of our liberty in Christ. Receiving Christ as Saviour provides the presence of His Spirit and, "...where the Spirit of the Lord is; there is liberty." (II Corinthians 3:17) Once again in Romans chapter eight Paul gives us clues to the nature of this liberty in progressive terms. **First**, we are free from the penalty of sin. Romans 8:1 declares, "There is therefore now no condemnation to them which are in Christ Jesus...." This is an immediate consequence of one's faith in Christ for salvation (the granting of His pardon). Jesus read from Isaiah 61:1 and said He was the fulfillment of this prophecy which included bringing liberty to the captives. Never will I worry that double jeopardy will be imposed upon me for the crimes now forgiven and under the blood of Jesus. I'm free from the guilt of the past, the fear of tomorrow and the uncertainty of today. **Second**, we are free from the power of sin. Three times in Romans chapter six Paul states that we who are pardoned are free from sin (vs. 7,18 &22) but this freedom is claimed on a daily basis by learning to yield to the Spirit rather than the flesh. The challenge presented in chapter eight is to walk after the Spirit and not the flesh. Since we have been set free from the reign of the flesh, we have the liberty to surrender to the authority of the Spirit of God who dwells within us. Don't let Flip Wilson convince you that the devil made you do it. As a child of God and with the Holy Spirit abiding in you, we are able to defeat the fiery darts of the devil, for greater is He that is within you than he that is in the world (I John 4;4). And **Third**, we will be set free from the very presence of sin. If the first stage of freedom from sin truly is freedom from the penalty of sin, that could be identified with the biblical term (*justification*), the second stage or freedom from the power of sin would be identified by the term (*sanctification*) which brings us to this stage of freedom from the presence of sin and the term *(glorification)*.

> *"Since we have been set free from the reign of the flesh, we have the liberty to surrender to the authority of the Spirit of God who dwells within us."*

There is coming a day when no heartache shall come, no more clouds in the sky and no more tears to dim the eye, no sickness, no pain and thank God no more sin. I disappoint myself daily by caving to the lust of the flesh, the lust of the eyes and the pride of life. If I had been Adam, I would have brought this fatal sentence on to mankind in just as short order as did Adam. I am acutely aware of my failings and my frailty. I am under no illusion of some superior status; but, one day I shall be like Him for I will see Him as He is and what a day of rejoicing that will be.

The Longevity of This Pardon

We live in a disposable world where nothing is intended to last: houses, appliances, cars, tools and even relationships are perishable. The life span of a lifetime warranty is until you leave the office or dealership. Forever lasts until the thrill is gone and a handshake doesn't count for a contract. Philadelphia lawyers have instilled such fine print that no one understands or believes the legitimacy of a promise. God is different. There shall not fail one word of all that He has promised. (See Joshua 21:45, Isaiah 55: 8-13 & I Kings 8:56) There is no more critical matter or important promise in the whole world than the promise of God concerning our Pardon. If there should be someone of higher rank that could veto or over-rank God's pardon, then we can never rest in God's promise. If the passing of enough time could annul God's pardon, then we are in constant peril. If God is so fickle that His word is not trustworthy then we have nothing sacred and/or solid to build upon. But, the Psalmist said, "Forever, O Lord, thy word is settled in heaven." (Psalm 119:89) In matters of judgement and the contract that God had with Israel, Malachi records the message from the Lord in Malachi 3:6, "For I am the LORD, I change not; therefore ye sons of Jacob are not consumed." Although the grace of God may be frustrated, (See Galatians 2:21) the pardon of God can never be revoked. The wise king Solomon penned that "...whatsoever God doeth, it shall be forever: nothing can be put to it, nor anything taken from it: and God doeth it, that men should fear before Him." (Ecclesiastes 3:14) I have been focusing on the legal language of the Apostle Paul found in Romans chapter eight. This great section of scripture provides the answer to the question of How Long? In terms of God's love and our pardon. "Who shall separate us from the love of Christ? shall tribulation, or distress, or persecution, or famine, or nakedness, or peril, or sword? As it is written, For thy sake we are killed all the day long; we are accounted as sheep for the slaughter. Nay, in all these things we are more than conquerors through Him that loved us. For I am persuaded, that neither death, nor life, nor angels, nor principalities, nor powers, nor things present, nor things to come, Nor height, nor depth, nor any other creature, shall be able to separate us from the love of God, which is in Christ Jesus our Lord." (Romans 8:35-39)

When I think about the purpose of Christ's coming to earth, repeated themes from the Bible come to mind. Luke records that Christ came to seek and to save that which was lost (Luke 19:10). Paul declared that Christ Jesus came into the world to save sinners... (I Timothy 1:15). And I especially enjoy singing the old hymn of Reverend George Bennard, entitled "The Old Rugged Cross" penned in 1913 and included in almost every hymn book compiled since then. When I come to the third verse my praise meter soars and I often pause and weep for... In the Old Rugged Cross, stained with blood so divine, a wondrous beauty I see; for 'twas on that old cross Jesus suffered and died to **pardon** and sanctify me. So, I'll cherish the old rugged cross, till my trophies at last I lay down; I will cling to the old rugged cross, and exchange it someday for a crown.

My prayer: Heavenly Father, I acknowledge my sin, my guilt and the price that I should pay for my sin. I deserve no consideration for Your mercy, and I am not worthy of Your pardon. I bow before You humbled and thankful for a place in Your kingdom and for my liberty in Christ. In the lovely name of Your Son Jesus I pray, Amen.

Chapter Two
KNOWING HIM IN HIS PERSON

Isaiah 1:3 "The ox knoweth his owner, and the ass his master's crib: but Israel doth not know, my people doth not consider."

Every journey begins with a first step and that first step may not even be a physical one. It is said concerning addicts of any kind that half the battle (the first half) is admitting that they have a problem. I propose that a similar truth exist about knowing the LORD. Knowing Him, I mean really knowing Him, does not happen accidentally and it cannot be absorbed through osmosis. However, if you are willing and committed to make this journey you should be prepared for spectacular scenery with breath taking views; an adventure that has a destination that is out of this world. One day when my journey ends, I will dwell in a place where I shall "know even as I am known." (I Corinthians 13:12) "I shall know Him and redeemed by His side I shall stand…." I came to know the LORD in 1962 and although many decades have passed, I still do not know Him as I should. Is not knowing Him a real problem? My answer is yes! Many folks throughout history have trivialized the knowledge of the LORD. In Exodus chapter five, Pharaoh would ask "Who is the LORD that I should obey His voice to let Israel go? I know not the LORD, neither will I let Israel go." He found out the hard way.

God wants to be known not because of His ego but because of the enormous good and bountiful love He has to bestow. James challenges us to draw nigh to God and in so doing, the distance between God and man is exponentially reduced because He in turn draws near to us (James 4:8). When phrases are repeated in the Bible, it gets my attention. Imagine how interested I became when I discovered that there were ninety-four places in the Bible that read, "know that I am the LORD" and sixty-four of them are in the same book (Ezekiel). Many of these occurrences speak of knowing Him through judgement but that is certainly not God's primary objective. He wants to be known and invites all to seek Him and begin this journey. In Jeremiah's prophecy of a restored Israel, he recorded a message from the LORD about a coming day when, "...they shall teach no more every man his neighbor and every man his brother, saying, Know the LORD: for they shall all know me, from the least of them unto the greatest of them, saith the LORD: for I will forgive their iniquity, and I will remember their sin no more." (Jeremiah 31:34) "What a day that will be..." but until that day let's commit ourselves to study to "know Him."

There really is a difference between knowing about Him and knowing Him. In fact, there are numerous ways to get to "know Him" and with each lesson we come to understand the character and heart of our loving, just, holy and unchanging God. The greatest stench in the nostrils of God just may be that we are at ease and content to not grow in our knowledge of Him. Those that knew Him far better than I do admonished us to grow in our knowledge of Him. They were not content with their superior level of knowledge. Peter once declared "with an oath, 'I do not know the man'." (Matthew 26:72) But this same Peter would leave the Bible narrative with this last recorded message, "But grow in grace, and in the knowledge of our Lord and Saviour Jesus Christ. To him be glory both now and forever. Amen." (II Peter 3:18) If you think you know enough, you don't know anything like you ought to know. See I Corinthians 8:2

In my over sixty-six years as a pilgrim here, I can count on my two hands the number of times I wasn't in church on the Lord's Day. That of course is a credit to my Godly parents. It was never an option or a question where we would be on Sunday, and I never resented it. All my friends were there, even the girls that I took a liken to were there. Growing up in a Godly home is a cherished blessing for me. And while growing up in the house of God may increase the odds of knowing Him, it doesn't provide a guarantee. Many of America's most wanted criminals or incarcerated convicts grew up in a Christian home attending church on a regular basis. Unfortunately, most of them never genuinely got to "know Him." The prophet Samuel grew up in the house of God but the Bible states, "Now Samuel did not yet know the LORD..." (I Samuel 3:7). Israel while enjoying the distinction of being God's chosen people and in a covenant relationship with Him failed miserably and for that complacency God raised up Isaiah to verbally scold them. This dis-interest in knowing Him was the cause for the book of Isaiah and it is immediately addressed. God's indictment against Israel is this, "The ox knoweth his owner, and the ass his master's crib: but Israel doth not know, my people doth not consider" (Isaiah 1:3). I am persuaded and the evidence is staggering that born again, washed in the blood children of God are guilty of not knowing their father nor are we inclined to "know Him." God forgive us this apathy.

There are three degrees or depths of knowledge considered in the word of God. We will briefly consider all three.

Knowing Him Intellectually

There is a small Greek word "ειδο" [eido #1492 in Strong's Concordance] or a form of it that is used 664 times in the New Testament. It is most often translated "to know" but with the concept that this knowledge comes from seeing. In fact, the Latin word "video" is derived from this little Greek word. It carries the idea of "taking notice of" or doing a double take to make sure you really saw what you think you saw. This is the degree or level of knowledge that Nicodemus demonstrated when he came to Jesus saying, "Rabbi <u>we know</u> that thou art a teacher come from God: for no man can do these miracles that thou doest, except God be with him." (John 3:2) Nicodemus was willing to acknowledge Him for what he had seen but by his own admission he had never experienced the new birth. Jesus actually challenged him by asking, "Art thou a master of Israel, and knowest not these things?" (John 3:10b) To this level of knowledge have many lost people come only to leave disappointed and retreat unchanged by this divine encounter. Knowing about Him or even taking a good look at Him will not suffice on judgment day. Many lost people possess this knowledge, they have been introduced to the Lord and may have even seen Him at work. The devil and his demons know intellectually the person of God and His son Jesus Christ, but to no avail. James, the half- brother of Jesus called attention to this deficiency when he recorded: "Thou believest (knowest) that there is one God; thou doest well: the devils also believe (know) and tremble." (James 2:19) Luke, the gospel writer and co-missionary with Paul even records the words of a demon in Acts chapter nineteen rebuking the pretentious sons of Sceva saying, "Jesus I know, and Paul I know; but who are ye?" Knowing Jesus intellectually and not experientially reminds me of a gospel tract that I read and distributed as a young man. The tract was entitled "Missing Heaven by 18 Inches." The obvious premise of the tract was that a head knowledge is inadequate and no substitute for a heart knowledge.

Knowing Him Experientially

Have you ever pondered the tremendous advantage of being an eyewitness of the many miracles of Christ, or hearing Him as He taught the learned scribes, pharisees, lawyers and philosophers of His day? What a joy it must have been to see, hear, touch or be touched by Jesus. But to Bethsaida, home to several apostles, or Nazareth the Lord's childhood home, or Capernaum the headquarters of Jesus' Galilean ministry, or for the young man with great possessions, or Pilate, or Judas; those privileges availed them nothing. Your knowledge of Christ must surpass theirs to have an eternal home in heaven. There is another Greek word translated "know" which is of a greater capacity the word is "γινωσκω" [(ginosko) #1097 in Strong's Concordance] This word carries the idea of knowing because of a place of common experience. Strong's Exhaustive Concordance of the Bible defines the word with the concept of understanding, like having a language in common. This knowledge could be described by Paul as his Roman Road experience, or by the Samaritan woman as her experience at the well. This kind of knowledge is only available to the saved, born again, "I've been to Calvary" kind of people. Interestingly, John uses this word to identify truly changed people who are walking in Christ' likeness obedient to His commandments. Without this kind of knowledge, you can talk and pretend but John says you are "a liar and the truth is not in" you. (I John 2:3-4)

> *"...really knowing Him, does not happen accidentally and it cannot be absorbed through osmosis."*

It is a shame that our world is full of people that have an intellectual knowledge of Christ. They have heard of Him, or they could pick Him out of a line-up. But they have never known Him by experience. Thankfully there are some who know Him having experienced His forgiveness of sin and by faith placed their hope in the finished work of Christ at Calvary. This kind of knowledge will suffice to take you to heaven; but there is a more thorough kind of knowledge. The kind of knowledge that will bring heaven down to you. A significantly smaller number of people have reached this peak of knowledge that calms through the storm, loves the unlovely, forgives the unforgivable, finds contentment with the meager, and gives thanks for the undesired.

Knowing Him Intimately

Our modern vernacular exclusively uses intimacy to describe some physical, sensual encounter that provides a temporary gratification which is selfish and illusive. The intimacy that the Lord desires is different and superior to that. This knowledge is intimate and intuitive. It is knowing Him so well that you think like Him and act like Him and grow to look more like Him. It mirrors the connection obtained between a man and his wife when after many years he can finish her sentences for her. He knows what she is thinking even when she says nothing at all. There is a phenomenon that I have noticed where a husband and wife can actually start to look like one another. The apostle Paul uses a word that reveals this level of knowledge. The Greek word is "επιγνοσις" (epignosis) and is used to define a full discernment or knowledge. (#1922 in Strong's Concordance) This word is used in Ephesians 4:13 and is connected to the perfect or mature man and reaching the measure of the fulness of Christ. It is most assuredly a knowledge that comes from deliberate attention or study of a subject and a fascination with every discovery. The Lord has nothing to hide about His nature or essence. He has no skeletons in His closet. You have nothing to worry about in learning the Lord. In fact, the more you know Him the more you will love Him.

On the occasion of my 25th wedding anniversary, I worried over what to get my wife. I finally decided to bite the bullet and ask what she would really like. In just a moment she gave me her response, "What I would really like is a bouquet of my favorite flowers." I was on the edge of my seat waiting for the qualifying information that was to follow; but there was nothing. In my embarrassment, it dawned on me that I probably should know this. I was able to search through enough photos that I correctly guessed, (yellow roses) sparing me a whole lot of penance. I have known the LORD for over 60 years, and I am still discovering wonderful things that I should have known long ago.

When Jeremiah prophesied of a restored Israel, he quoted the LORD saying, "AND I WILL GIVE THEM AN HEART TO KNOW ME, THAT I AM THE LORD: AND THEY SHALL BE MY PEOPLE, AND I WILL BE THEIR GOD: FOR THEY SHALL RETURN UNTO ME WITH THEIR WHOLE HEART" (24:7) During Elihu's indictment against Job, (Job 36:26) he blankly states that "God is great, and we know Him not..." This is the real charge against modern Christianity. But the charge is at least in two counts. First that we know Him not, and second that we are content for that to remain the case. If the status quo bothers you like it does me, it can be fixed.

My prayer, "Father I acknowledge my shallow and superficial interest in you and your divine essence. Please forgive me this wrong and create in me a heart to study you, to learn you, to know you that I may love and serve you as I should. In Jesus name I pray, Amen."

Chapter Three

KNOWING HIM IN HIS PEACE

John 16:33 "These things I have spoken unto you, that in me ye might have peace. In the world ye shall have tribulation: but be of good cheer; I have overcome the world."

For anyone growing up in the 1960's, those were unforgettable years. The assassination of a president, the deployment of U.S. troops to America's most unpopular war and bell bottom pants. The decade is also well known for the birth of a counterculture known as the "hippies." Their anti-war slogans and anti-establishment rhetoric were symbolized by tie-dye shirts, bandannas, flowers and peace symbols. I later learned that the peace symbol was designed to disgrace the cross (upside down and broken). But who in his right mind would not embrace "PEACE"? Looking back, this crowd resembled one that Jeremiah witnessed and described as an audience of false prophets, saying, "Peace, peace; when there is no peace." The question could and should be raised, Will there ever be genuine peace? The answer is an emphatic YES! A rightful subsequent question would then be, when will this peace come? The answer to that question is, when Jesus, the Son of God, reigns supreme.

The word "peace" is used 429 times in the King James Bible. Is the word used just to tease us with the unobtainable? Is it a dangling carrot that remains just out of reach? No, this illusive peace seems impossible because of the wicked hearts of mankind. The year 2020 will likely go down in history as a year of unrest, unruly mobs and mass destruction. There is no peace in sight. Since time began or more precisely since the fall of man, peace has been short lived at best. The Bible records peace for Israel during the days of Solomon (960 -920 BC) as Israel's king. (See I Chronicles 22:9 and I Kings 4:24-25) Solomon's father David did not experience it and his son Rehoboam didn't either. America has only known peace in short periods. The prospects for the future may be dismal also, for the LORD said that "wars and rumors wars" would be a way of life for the last days. (Matthew 24:6)

A wise man once said, "Know Jesus, Know Peace; No Jesus, No Peace." Isaiah identified the LORD as the "Prince of Peace." (Isaiah 9:6) The word Prince denotes the head or chief officer and as such He reigns over peace. Peace is subject to Him and apart from Him there is only chaos, turmoil and strife. The chaos that America is experiencing today is a direct result of dethroning and evicting God from our society. We are reaping the consequences of the seeds we have sown. Conversely, the Psalmist declares, "Blessed is the nation whose God is the LORD" (Psalm 33:12) The Lord identified as guardian and giver of peace when He said, "These things I have spoken unto you, that in me ye might have peace. In the world ye shall have tribulation: but be of good cheer; I have overcome the world." (John 16:33) Therefore, true peace is not the absence of a storm but the presence of the Lord.

On the evening of the Lord's betrayal and arrest, the Apostle John records that our Lord was preparing and encouraging His disciples for His departure. He was particularly identifying how He would continue to care for them once absent in body. He said, "Peace I leave with you, my peace I give unto you: not as the world giveth, give I unto you. Let not your heart be troubled neither let it be afraid." (John 14:27) The Baptist theologian of the eighteenth century, John Gill, said that John 14:27 records "the last will and testament of Jesus." Let that sink in; the Lord's disciples, including me, are the benefactors of His amazing peace. I get to know and experience His peace. I don't have to be troubled or afraid. To examine the Lord's peace reveals that He was never anxious about anything. His peace is the kind that can cause you to endure the cross for the sake of the coming joy. That kind of peace was present with Daniel in the den of lions. It allowed Stephen to endure stoning while looking into the face of Jesus, enabled Paul to face beheading, Peter to bear his cross, our fore-fathers to be burned at the stake and my dear mother to die with a smile on her face and a stare in her eyes toward eternity.

When Jesus said, "my peace", there are at least two claims that we must consider. The first is the peace He owns and the second is the peace He enjoys. The Lord owns peace by virtue of creation. Everything, tangible or intangible is subject to Him because He made it. He commands the winds and the waves, and they obey Him. They must, they have no power of their own. The disciples were amazed to discover this truth while the violent waves and the boisterous winds beat on their ship. When they in fear awakened the Lord to their dilemma, Jesus said "Peace be still." What had been a life and death struggle was made of no consequence when Jesus spoke peace. This calls attention to the second of the claims. Jesus not only is Lord over peace, but He is also always enjoying this peace. Jesus was never startled or wringing his hands over the circumstances He faced or the environment of oppressors. No matter what it looked like on the surface, Jesus never resorted to "plan B." Under Roman oppression, religious bias, rejection and even betrayal, Jesus remained at perfect peace (see Isaiah 26:3). Before Pontius Pilate and a mob of false witnesses, Jesus kept His calm. Jesus had the power to control and/or change His circumstances, He chose rather to control His response to those circumstances. We have that same privilege if we so choose. After the crucifixion and resurrection of Christ, upon His first appearance to His disciples He spoke these familiar words, "Peace be unto you." (Luke 24:36) Although the disciples were in need of a refresher course, history commends them for having finally understood His peace and they all faced their giants with courage and calm until their death.

The use of three different prepositions in connection with "peace" exposes three different characteristics or levels of God's peace:

PEACE WITH GOD

This is a foundational kind of peace. Man because of his sinful nature and his sinful practice is at enmity with God. We are enemies, on the wrong side standing in opposition to God. Man can never experience peace with God in this setting. Something drastic must happen, a new birth. Paul refers to this level of peace in Romans 5:1 "Therefore being justified by faith, we have peace with God through our Lord Jesus Christ." Again, in Ephesians 2:13-14 Paul states, "But now in Christ Jesus ye who sometimes were far off are made nigh by the blood of Christ. For he is our peace, who hath made both one, and hath broken down the middle wall of partition between us." What a thrill to have made peace with our maker and not have to live under the shadow of His wrath, with God as our enemy. This peace bridges the great divide between Man and God. Jesus himself becoming that bridge.

PEACE FROM GOD

This divine gift is a steppingstone of peace intended to create a bridge between Man and Man. It is exhibited in the soft answer of a child of God or the ability to be wronged without recourse. Easier said than done to not strike back. As much as it is part of the human nature to want to settle the score, to avenge yourself, to get even, to give them a piece of your mind (the wrong piece), it is equally a part of the divine nature to forgive, to suffer wrong, to prefer one another, to love your enemies. This is the message and the model of Christ and is available to every believer through the peace we have obtained from God. I am not condoning the sacrifice of our integrity or the surrender of our faith, not at all; never deny Him or back away from those things most surely believed among us; but to answer Paul's beseeching to "as much as lieth in you, live peaceably with all men." (Romans 12:18) Some folks who claim to be Christians display anything but a Christlike temperament. They may not always be right, but they will always be heard, even if it is stirring up strife. Jesus said, "offenses will come but woe unto him, through whom they come!" (Luke 17:1) The Apostle John spoke of peace from God in II John 1:3 and it is this level of peace from God that enables you to walk together in truth and to love one another. Knowing the wrong and injustice that Christ endured should compel us to take this step in our knowledge of Him in His peace. Paul, the apostle to the Gentiles opened every letter that he claimed authorship with the words "...and peace from God..." in his salutation.

PEACE OF GOD

This concept and level of peace is intended to build a bridge between the natural man and the God man that lives within us. This internal strife is not a new phenomenon, the scriptures speak often of this conflict. It is not intended to make you tolerant of sin, or complacent with mediocrity but to anoint you with balm on your way to Christlikeness. "For a just man falleth seven times, and riseth up again..." (Proverbs 24:16) God used Paul to pen one of my favorite verses in the Bible, Philippians 4:7 reads, "And the peace of God, which passeth all understanding, shall keep your hearts and minds through Christ Jesus." I don't yet understand it but I acknowledge it and am trying to enjoy this peace of God on my way home. It has been my joy to lead many expeditions, pilgrimages or maybe just tours to Israel. I have tried to prepare those who are traveling with me for some unusual realities. For instance, you may see teen-agers (soldiers) on the street with large semi-automatic or automatic weapons. For us this would be shocking but for them a way of life. I generally tell them to look into my eyes, if I don't look worried then you have no reason to be worried either. If you will look into the eyes of the Lord you will see that He is not now nor has he ever been worried about the outcome of any circumstance we have or will ever face. Just trust Him, He's got this.

"Peace is not the absence of a storm, but the presence of the Lord"

Looking back on John 14, I noticed that Jesus said, "I leave…I give unto you…" and calls attention to the difference between His gift of peace and that of the world. There is a difference in the gift as we have already addressed, but there is also a difference in the giving. The world throws peace around as an empty salutation much like the hippies did. We say, "How are you?" and really don't care. We say, "Good day" and really don't mean it. Jesus was pouring Himself into the disciples' future and promising them an unexplainable peace. His giving was deliberate, intentional and thorough. The Jewish culture recognized "Shalom" as a customary greeting which of course means peace, but as Jesus used the word in this setting, it was not as a salutation but as a treasured family heirloom, something bequeathed, a valuable commodity. The Greek word that is used here is "ειρηνην" translated "peace" from a higher degree or level of peace and speaks of oneness, rest, quiet and prosperity. This peace exists regardless of circumstances and only in Christ. This peace is ours in Christ and we should crave it, pray for it, strive diligently for it and not be satisfied until we know Him in His peace. And if you need more reason to desire this peace, I would like to share one more reason why we should pursue this peace. Because of the price He paid for it.

For mankind to have peace with God, cost God His son. He allowed Him to be made sin for us, not a sinner, but sin. God could not wholesale sin's price just because His son was paying. The price was great. Have you ever read Isaiah 53 looking through the lens of our debt? Consider the depths of God's love and the supreme price paid for our redemption and the ability to have "peace with God." Isaiah put it this way, "But he was wounded for our transgressions, he was bruised for our iniquities: **the chastisement of our peace was upon him;** and with his stripes we are healed." The chastisement or discipline or condition of our peace was upon Him. He is our only hope. Had He not come, paid our debt, fulfilled the law and satisfied the demands of our Holy father, we would be hopeless in our sins and remained enemies of God on our way to the torment we deserve.

People who know me well are aware of the place that music has in my life. I think of a song for almost every occasion. I have a tendency to sing when I should be quiet. But songs touch me, and God uses them to calm my spirit. I often reflect on the childhood songs that I learned for youth camp or Vacation Bible School. One such song has a great verse that goes like this: "I have the peace that passeth understanding down in my heart... down in my heart to stay. If the devil doesn't like it, he can sit on a tack. You get the picture.

Is the lack of peace a real problem? Today, globally there is an epidemic of anxiety and a plethora of available prescriptions to treat this condition. Routinely advertised on the television are: Pristiq, Lexapro, Zoloft, Prozac, Effexor XR, Paxil CR, Abilify, Celexa, Xanax, Valium, Tofranil, Remoran, Cymbalta, Ativan, Klonopin, and Norpramin; these medications generate billions of dollars in revenue for the pharmacies. There are also many ways to treat this anxiety, including Psychotherapy, Aromatherapy, Hypnotism, Yoga and even Calgon. As a last hope why not try Christ, who is the guardian and giver of peace.

My prayer: Father, I have found it easy to be trouble and afraid. I have watched the winds and waves and taken my eyes off of you. Please forgive me, open my eyes like you did for Elisha's servant. Help my mind to be stayed on thee that I may enjoy perfect peace. In Jesus name, Amen.

The photo below was taken around September of 1960. It is hard to believe that my parents could have known how precious this little book would be to me. Or maybe they prayed, believing that someday I would grasp the beauty of Christ as painted in the Book. If this was their prayer, it took about 50 years, but the LORD honored their prayer and the love for the Bible I observed in them. I remain fascinated that the Jesus I saw on the cover, I found painted on every page inside as well.

Chapter Four
KNOWING HIM IN THE PAGES

II Timothy 3:14-17 "But continue thou in the things which thou hast learned and hast been assured of, knowing of whom thou hast learned them; And that from a child thou hast known the Holy Scriptures, which are able to make thee wise unto salvation through faith which is in Christ Jesus. All Scripture is given by inspiration of God, and is profitable for doctrine, for reproof, for correction, for instruction in righteousness: That the man of God may be perfect, throughly furnished unto all good works."

Many years ago, I heard a story, probably not a true one, about a rich atheist that offered a young boy a dollar if the boy could show the rich man "where God is." Without missing a beat, the young boy responded, "I am obviously not as old as you, I may not be as smart as you and I am certainly not as rich as you; but I will give you a hundred dollars if you can show me where He ain't." Since God is omni-present, He is in all places simultaneously. (See Psalm 139:7-12) When I look into the heavens, I see the canvas of His artwork and the testimony of His greatness. I find myself reciting the words of the Psalmist, David, "The heavens declare the glory of God; and the firmament showeth His handiwork." (Psalm 19:1) I join in with the choir that sings, "O Lord my God, when I in awesome wonder, consider all the worlds thy hands have made. I see the stars; I hear the rolling thunder; Thy power throughout the universe displayed. Then sings my soul, 'My Saviour God to Thee' How Great Thou Art, How Great Thou Art." Can you imagine the brand-new galaxies that Adam investigated on his first unpolluted evening, about six thousand years ago? He knew he was staring into the creator's majestic tapestry. Then the Master revealed His heavenly gospel through constellations and the first connect the dots game was created.

Is the Bible the only source for the knowledge of God? Absolutely not. God has revealed Himself through many realms. Romans chapter one shares that man is without excuse even without a Bible. (See Romans 1:18-25) A science teacher friend of mine sparked my interest in astronomy and I have been richly blessed to study this science. I have even more so enjoyed the revelation of "the bright and morning star" (Revelation 22:16) and like Paul discovered that the light of the Son is brighter than the sun. To the horticulturist or botanist, He is the "Rose of Sharon" and the "Lily of the Valley." For the anatomist, David shared that we are "fearfully and wonderfully made" and that God has an infinite knowledge of all our parts, even before they were assembled. (Psalm 139:1-16) If you are a geologist then you should be interested to know that the mountains move for Him, He holds the earth's waters in the hollow of His hand. The rocks are on stand-by to cry out His praises. He spoke the world into being, it is His handiwork. If zoology is your thing, I have good news for you because even the animal kingdom acknowledges Him. A donkey once yielded himself to become a spokesman for God when the prophet Balaam was traveling down the wrong road. On another occasion a donkey stood ready and offered his back to Jesus for His triumphal entry into Jerusalem. God employed a rooster to deliver one of the most scathing messages ever preached. Not to mention the sparrows that humbly rely on His provision. Isaiah recorded the message of an angel who said, "...the whole earth is full of His glory." (Isaiah 6:3)

Although you can study and/or get knowledge of the Lord from astronomy, anatomy, botany, geology, zoology and any number of other mind fields; the absolute, most profound resource for revelation of Jesus Christ is the Holy Bible. The Word of God is an impeccable error free Biography of God's son, Jesus. The Bible provides the history of Christ, in fact, it is His-Story. The

Bible is a living book, and it is so because of its relevance to all generations and that is true because, the subject, meets every person's greatest need for all times. Any pursuit of the knowledge of Christ that relies on a textbook other than the Bible will produce an inferior knowledge. Sometimes I am so dense that I need a picture drawn for me. God has done just that, many times over. An oft repeated idiom is, "a picture is worth a thousand words (not a Bible verse). Through "Google Search" I discovered that there are 783,137 words in my Bible, so by my math there should be, and I am sure there are 783 great pictures or illustrations of Jesus in the sacred book. I haven't found them all yet, but I have marveled at those I have discovered. There are several books available on the types and shadows of Christ found in scripture. Many of these pictures are painted in the Old Testament and exposed in the New Testament. For instance, the rock that Moses struck in the wilderness which gushed out water to satisfy the wandering Israelites, was Jesus. (I Corinthians 10:4) A small sampling of these types (pictures) of Christ could include: Noah's Ark, the Passover lamb and even the serpent that Moses raised upon a pole. My heart leaps with joy as I walk through the art gallery of the Old Testament.

> "The Bible provides the history of Christ, in fact, it is His-Story"

The fact that the Bible is a photo album of Jesus is evidenced in the New Testament. Two locations particularly identify this truth. In John chapter five and in Luke chapter twenty-four Jesus himself stakes the claim. In John's account, Jesus is providing a defense for His claim of deity. John 5:39 reads, "Search the Scriptures; for in them ye think ye have eternal life: and they are they which testify of me." And just a few verses later Jesus said, "For had ye believed Moses, ye would have believed me: for he wrote of me. But if ye believe not his writings, how shall ye believe my words?" (John 5:46-47) In Luke's record, Jesus provided other evidence of this truth. Jesus, on the day of His resurrection, joins a couple of His disciples on the Emmaus

Road and He explains the events of the preceding days from Moses' writings and then from the writings of other prophets. He said what they wrote was about me. (See Luke 24:25-32 & 44-46). These two references indicate that had those respective audiences really applied themselves they could have seen Jesus and known what was happening. Jesus identified himself as the main character of the Old Testament manuscripts. There are at least three distinct benefits of knowing Jesus through the pages of scripture.

Knowing Him in the Pages Reaps Faith and Service

If you are satisfied with your level or degree of faith, if your service to God has reached its summit then don't read your Bible. The consequential response to Bible study is faith and the result of faith is service. Paul expressed this truth to the saints in Rome by saying, "So then faith cometh by hearing, and hearing by the word of God." (Romans 10:17) To read of the mighty works of God; to know how He showed up and how victory was won for our forefathers has a way of inciting us to expect God to do it again. He is after all the same yesterday, today and forever. (Hebrews 13:8) Every generation should be the beneficiary of the testimony from the preceding generation. To hear of the great things that Christ has done and how He has answered prayer. When a generation fails to pass that on, the collective faith of the next generation wanes. New Testament saints benefited from the faith displayed by Old Testament saints. Men like Job, Daniel and Elijah whose faith delivered them from their perils blazed a trail for New Testament saints to travel. These saints were not likely conscious of the legacy that they would leave behind, but their faith challenged others and the chain of the faithful was linked from Old Testament to New Testament and unto the modern day faithful. One great reason to read Hebrews chapter eleven is to see faith in action and it is even possible to see it move from one generation to the next. Abraham is known as, "the father of the faithful" partly because his faith was replicated in his son and again in his grandson. There are three different demands from God with regards to our connection to the Word. The first is to "search the Scriptures", the second is to "study the Scriptures" and the third is to "secure the Scriptures." This last one implies the idea of burying, depositing or hiding which is exactly what the Psalmist said he would do.

Knowing Him in the Pages Reduces Our Falling into Sin

While searching and studying will directly impact your faith and service; the securing of the Word is the resource and the reserve that meets the emergent threat of falling into sin. If you have ever put money into a jar or put a little something away for a rainy day, then you might understand the concept expressed in Psalm 119:11. "Thy word have I hid in my heart, that I might not sin against Thee." There is no island so remote that living there will free you from the hour of temptation. No monk or hermit is so secluded that they cannot feel the chilling draft of the devil's winds. Even Jesus himself was tempted. (Matthew 4:1-11) The Bible clearly teaches that temptation is a common denominator of humanity (see I Corinthians 10:13). It is not a sin to be tempted; temptation is the empty promise of the devil; lying that real peace, joy and happiness comes through rebellion to Christ or perhaps just taking a slight detour from God's path for our lives. By our study of the Bible, two wonderful things happen. First, we find the sweet and blessed path of those who denied themselves and the pleasure of sin for a season (see Hebrews 11:25); and second, we find the fall-out, folly and failures of those that made their own path. "There is a way which seemeth right unto a man, but the end thereof are the ways of death." (Proverbs 14:12)

So how do we avoid this destruction and death? Through an embedded knowledge of the Lord and His word we can fight off the fiery darts of Satan. As Paul presented the "whole armor of God" to the saints at Ephesus, (Ephesians 6:17) he identified our offensive weapon (our sword) as the Word of God. It behooves us to be familiar with and even proficient with our sword against the inevitable day of battle. As we noticed earlier Christ was tempted, "...in all points tempted like as we are, yet without sin." (Hebrews 4:15) Our Lord's victory over temptation provides us with the best approach and what should be our strategy against temptation. On each occasion the devil tempted Jesus, and regardless of the gateway he approached Jesus, Jesus always responded with, "it is written." (Matthew 4:4,7 & 10) The Bible is much like our "Stand Your Ground" law that causes the perpetrator or invader to tuck tail and run or face an even worse fate. "...Resist the devil and he will flee from you." (James 4:7) God's Word in our heart is like the invisible force field that vaporizes the enemy's bullets that neutralizes the poisonous venom that is intended to destroy our lives and witness. The Old Testament prophet Isaiah records a message of the Lord for Israel that is yet to be fulfilled. It is true because the Lord said so but the condition that is provided is that the Lord has made a covenant with Israel. He said, "No weapon that is formed against thee shall prosper; and every tongue that shall rise against thee in judgment thou shall condemn. This is the heritage of the servants of the LORD, and their righteousness is of me, saith the LORD." (Isaiah 54:17) We can stay on the right path and avoid temptation's snare and/or the consequences of yielding to sin by hiding God's Word in our hearts. The Bible lights the right path and reveals the dangers along the way. (See Psalm 119:105) Either the Bible will keep you from sin, or sin will keep you from the Bible.

Knowing Him in the Pages Reveals the Fullness of the Son

The Bible was given and is preserved for us that we might Know Him. It is expected of us as His children that we would grow in our knowledge of Him and in our likeness of Him. Ephesians 4:13 reads, "Till we all come in the unity of the faith, and of the knowledge of the Son of God, unto a perfect man, unto the measure of the stature of the fullness of Christ:." Although the last book in the Bible is named "Revelation", it is not the only book intended to reveal Christ. Every picture in the Bible is there for our observation, consideration and assimilation of Jesus Christ. John recorded in his account of the Gospel that "the Word was made flesh... and of His fullness have all we received..." (see John 1:14-18) Jesus is the living Word and it stands to reason that the written word would be a description of Him.

God provided for Israel six special cities that would be recognized as "cities of refuge", a place where a man could flee that was trying to avoid an avenger of blood. If the judges of the city deemed that the offense of the one fleeing was not an act of premeditation or deliberation the city would welcome the offender into their city and provide refuge for them only so long as they remained in the city. But something strange happened in Israel upon the death of the High Priest, every offender protected by the city of refuge was freed and the avenger had no claim of retribution against them. That is more than just an interesting phenomenon in the history books of Israel, it is a picture of you and me guilty and secluded without any liberty until Christ, our High Priest, died and the message was delivered "all who are in refuge may go free." It is why the fig leaves were insufficient coverings for Adam and Eve in the garden. Though their bodies were covered their sin was still exposed. It was necessary that blood be shed for their sin covering. All the thousands of gallons of blood shed in sacrifice through the Old Testament was not because of God's hatred of animals, or some diabolical wicked fetish; but rather to remind the world of the cost of our sin ("...and sin, when it is finished, bringeth forth death." James 1:15) and the high price that would be required to pay our ransom.

> *"The Bible will keep you from sin, or sin will keep you from the Bible."* Dwight L. Moody

It would be the most rewarding study you have ever engaged, if you should look for the pictures of Jesus in the Bible and become fascinated with the divine purpose of the Book, The B-I-B-L-E yes that's the book for me. I read and pray and then obey, the B-I-B-L-E.

My prayer: My Father in heaven, your word which is so sharp that it divides soul and spirit, has become abused through neglect in my hands. Help me to search through the pearls of scripture that I might find the pearl of great price. Forgive my apathy of Your Word and help me to have the desire of those before me who said, "show me thy glory." Help me to love thy law and to seek You upon every page, In Jesus name, Amen.

Chapter Five
KNOWING HIM IN HIS PASSION

I John 4:16 "And we have known and believed the love that God hath to us. God is love; and he that dwelleth in love dwelleth in God, and God in him."

In 1946, ten years before my arrival, my father was a walk-on (undrafted) punter for the University of Miami. It did not materialize into a career, and it was actually a secret from my grandmother for most of her life. She would never have consented to her brittle baby boy being brutally beaten. Despite his short-lived dream, my father always remained a fan of the Edison High School and the University of Miami, his alma maters. I am not a graduate of UM, nor an alumnus of either of those schools; in fact, I have never set foot on either one of those campuses. Nonetheless, I consider myself a die-hard fan of the University of Miami for my father's sake. I think of my dad every time I see the green and orange "U" on display. My love for the institution is not a result of their unprecedented five national championships but because my father loved and played for them. Loving that school did not improve my football skills or even make me a better person but showing and demonstrating my allegiance does honor my dad and just maybe shows my love for him. I have the shirt, the mug, the football, the helmet, the tie, the quilt and even a Miami decorated golf cart. I am a real fan, and I don't mind if it shows.

It is said of King David, Israel's beloved king, that he was "a man after God's own heart." (I Samuel 13:14 & Acts 13:22) What if there is a suggestion in this statement that David was in pursuit of (after) God's heart rather than just of a similar type.

There is nothing insignificant or trivial about having a heart similar to God's heart, but that doesn't convey the concept of intention or purpose that is true of David. David wanted to capture the heart of God by developing a like passion. If you have ever been smitten by someone (hit by Cupid's arrow) to the point that you pursued and embraced their hobbies just so you could spend time with them, then you might be able to relate to King David's pursuit. David had fixed his heart on the LORD (Psalm 57:7 & 108:12) and God honored David's fixation with an intimate connection. If you will draw nigh to God, then He will draw nigh to you (See James 4:8). That is apparently what drove and motivated Kind David; setting him apart from all others and causing him to be recognized as Israel's greatest King and the standard by which all others would be judged.

If "to know Him is to love Him" is true, then the reverse may also be true; "to love Him is to know Him." There are eleven verses in the Bible that contain both "love" and "know" and there are five more verses that contain "love" and "knowledge" together. If you are truly passionate about knowing Him, then becoming passionate about the things He is passionate about is a good place to start. It is this ambition that prompted the gospel artist, David Ingles, in 1959 to write the hymn, "Love like the Love of God." We should be searching, praying, longing for a love like the love of God. One of the eleven occasions where love and know are used together is in Ephesians chapter three and verse nineteen. It was a passion of Paul's life to know the Lord; and, to bring others along on his life's pursuit. Paul's prayer for the saints in Ephesus was for them to know the Lord and the fullness of His love. Ephesians 3:14-19 reads, "For this cause I bow my knees unto the Father of our LORD Jesus Christ, Of whom the whole family in heaven and earth is named, That He would grant you, according to the riches of His glory, to be strengthened with might by His Spirit in the inner man; That Christ may dwell in your hearts by faith; that ye, being rooted and grounded in love, May be able to comprehend with all the saints what is the breadth, and length, and depth, and height; And to know the love of Christ, which passeth knowledge, that ye might be filled with all the fulness of God." Among "the unsearchable riches of Christ" (3:8) that Paul preached, was the multi-faceted, fathomless love of Christ. Paul wanted to know and cause others to know the breadth, length, depth, height, girth and weight of Christ' love; not just to be a recipient of but a participant in that kind of love. To know the love of Christ may demand of us that we study to discover the objects of our LORD's love. I am on a campaign to know Him that way and I am hoping you will join me. I cannot provide an unabridged, comprehensive list of all the things, places and people that have known the love of God; I am truly blessed that I am a recipient of that love. Considering the vastness of or the boundless nature of God's love exposes the narrowness of mine. Jesus asked His disciples what kind of reward do you expect for loving those who love you first, anybody can do that? (See Matthew 5:46) I feel compelled to focus attention on a few of the things no doubt on that list of things He loves, for His love is the perfect model of love.

His Passion for the Saints

I am impressed and positively impacted by Christ' love for his saints: saved folks, born again, blood washed and new creatures that carry around the old man, the carnal man. Accepting Christ as your personal savior doesn't always translate into being loveable. I have met many so-called Christians which have challenged my ability and even my desire to love. They can be down-right hateful. It is even possible that you or I might be that person at times. But Christ' command remains the same, unqualified and without an asterisk. Love them. This kind of love is a badge and when worn properly, it identifies us with the LORD. (See John 13:35) What a different world we would be living in if the love of Christ was to spread with the same speed and tenacity as COVID-19. Paul commended the saints in Ephesus for their "love unto all the saints" (2:15) and to him it was a trophy of the years he labored and ministered among them. Not only are the saints not always loveable, but they are also not always right. What should our response be to them then? Love saints the way the LORD loves you, even when you are wrong. There may be dozens of lessons learned from the parable of the prodigal son in Luke chapter 15, one of the greatest for me is that the father never quit loving the son. Even in disgrace or embarrassment the father always identified with and loved the son. Throughout the church age, the instruction for the church has been that discipline would be meted out in love. Love is the standard for all we do. It is not recorded that loving others would be easy, even loving the saints, but it is the right thing to do, it is the Christlike thing to do. Is this a big deal? I mean is loving my brother that important? The answer is found in I John chapter 4 and verse 20 which John penned through inspiration. "If a man say, I love God, and hateth his brother, he is a liar: for he that loveth not his brother whom he hath seen, how can he love God whom he hath not seen? All I can add to that is: Ouch!

His Passion for His Spouse

A second focus of Christ' love is the love He has directed toward His Church. True churches; chaste, robed in white, called out, fitted, knit and covenanted together, "The Bride of Christ." Paul called attention to this love in Ephesians 5:25, "Husbands, love your wives, even as Christ also loved the church, and gave Himself for it."

"Love is a badge, and when worn properly, it identifies us with the Lord".

There are many nuances to the Jewish wedding and the marriage supper that parallel with the betrothal and anticipated marriage of the Lamb. Among the greatest similarities is the depth and commitment level of this love and the preparation made for the big event. This is true of both husband and wife, and Jesus and His Church. Christ is the ultimate husband and loves with an uncompromising passion for His bride. Jesus possesses all the qualities of God the Father because He is in all points equal with the Father. If then God is love, so then Christ is love as well. The above verse shares that He gave Himself for the church. This selfless act of love has become the standard of genuine love. It demonstrates total surrender like a man dying for his wife, family, country or a cause, Jesus died for His bride.

His greatest expression is our greatest commandment. Love God and love others. If your life was examined and judged for your love of His church, how would you fare? Does your faithful attendance, your cheerful contribution and dedicated service match your claim of love for Christ? Would the world find you guilty of loving like Christ, based solely on what they examine in your love for the church? Every member of the body (church) is distinct, different and diverse in function or purpose; but still one body. My leg has never had a falling out with my arm, instead they have learned to cooperate and work together in harmony. (See I Corinthians 12:12-27) The body can exist without an arm or a leg; however, it is greatly hampered in its achievements. It is probably true that many hands make light work, but not if they are not connected to the arm or brought to the job by the legs. God knows what He is doing when He teams up saints in the harness together. Work together until you learn to love one another as Christ loves the church.

His Passion for Lost Souls

The golden text of the Bible is undoubtedly John 3:16 and this reference has been displayed on business cards, billboards and athletes charcoal painted faces. The most memorized verse of the Bible reveals God's love for the world, the wandering lost, the destitute in need of a savior. At least three other verses reveal that the purpose of Christ' coming was to seek and save the lost. (See Matthew 18:11, Luke 19:10 & I Timothy 1:15) The majority of Ephesians chapter two is dedicated to the subject of salvation and the tremendous expense associated with our redemption and our Lord's willingness to pay that price with His own blood. In Ephesians 2:4 Paul calls attention to Christ's "...great love wherewith He loved us." It was this passion for the lost that necessitated Jesus' journey through Samaria (John 4:4-42) where He encountered the woman that needed more than a bucket of water. And it was His love that caused Him to take the trip to Tyre/Sidon where He met a woman desperate for the healing of her possessed daughter. Jesus met that need, healed her daughter and bragged on her faith. (Matthew 15:21-28 & Mark 7:24-30)

A preacher friend of mine claims that his favorite Bible verse is the five times it is recorded that "He was moved with compassion." The verse I have claimed as my life's verse is Jude 22 and I share it often. It reads, "And of some have compassion, making a difference." His compassions they fail not and if exercised correctly ours won't either. I probably don't have the best phone etiquette and sometimes it gets me in trouble, but one of my routines is to end each call with "I love you, Goodbye." That throws the annoying tele-marketer a curve ball, but sometimes it opens a door of opportunity for me to share why. I love you because Jesus loves you. I chose three words to guide my life and give purpose for my existence and then years later I created a little banner/business card that embraced those three words.

Directions for a Meaningful Life

It was this selfless spirit that caused Charles D. Meigs, around 1900, to pen the great poem,

"Others"

Lord help me live from day to day In such a self-forgetful way
That even when I kneel to pray My prayer shall be for – Others.
Help me in all the work I do To ever be sincere and true
And know that all I do for you Must needs be done for – Others.
Let "Self" be crucified and slain And buried deep; and all in vain
May efforts be to rise again Unless to live for – Others.
And when my work on earth is done And
my new work in heaven's begun
May I forget the crown I've won While thinking still of – Others.
Others, Lord, yes others Let this my motto be
Help me to live for others That I may live like Thee.

Some thirty years after Paul sent his letter to the Ephesian church, bragging on their love of the saints and sharing the overwhelming love of Christ for the church and the lost, the Apostle John would send another letter to them; this one not so warm and fuzzy. In thirty years, they had managed to leave their first love and the LORD called them out on it, reprimanding them for this falling away from the intensity in the cause He left them with. They had become lukewarm. Our marching orders are found in all of the gospels, but my favorite is found in John 20:21, "Then said Jesus to them again, Peace be unto you: as my Father hath sent me, even so send I you." If you love like the Lord loves, you will go and you will tell.

My prayer: Dear Father, You instructed me not to love the world or the things of this world, I have failed. You demanded of me to Love God and to love my neighbor as myself, I have failed. Please Father, enlarge my heart to love what you love and as you love, that I might know you more intimately and have a greater impact for You while on this, my journey home. In Jesus name, Amen.

Chapter Six
Knowing Him in His Punishment

Hebrews 12:5-11 "And ye have forgotten the exhortation which speaketh unto you as unto children, My son, despise not thou the chastening of the Lord, nor faint when thou art rebuked of Him: For whom the Lord loveth He chasteneth, and scourgeth every son whom He receiveth. If ye endure chastening, God dealeth with you as with sons; for what son is he whom the father chasteneth not? But if ye be without chastisement, whereof all are partakers, then are ye bastards, and not sons. Furthermore we have had fathers of our flesh which corrected us and we gave them reverence: shall we not much rather be in subjection unto the Father of spirits, and live? For they verily for a few days chastened us after their own pleasure; but He for our profit, that we might be partakers of His holiness. Now no chastening for the present seemeth to be joyous, but grievous: nevertheless afterward it yieldeth the peaceable fruit of righteousness unto them which are exercised thereby."

Without a doubt the least popular of all chapters in this study is this one. In fact, I had intended to include an appropriate hymn with each chapter; but I haven't been able to find a song that deals with the subject of God's punishment. It is absolutely imperative that a Holy God demand holiness from His subjects. In fact, God is too Holy to look upon sin. There must be a consequence to our rebellion or our laxness to His demands. What strength does a command without an "or else" really have? It essentially becomes just a suggestion. The Bible is full of "if/then" statements. These are commandments with absolute consequences. You might notice for example Genesis 2:17 where God gave man the first such clause, if you eat of that tree then you die. But there are hundreds of them (Deuteronomy 28, II Chronicles 7:14, Isaiah 1:18–19) that demonstrate God's seriousness and commitment to hold us accountable to His demands.

God has always been a God of "punishment," His holiness demands it. Even before there was man there was punishment. Angels in rebellion to God faced and will face stiff punishment (Jude 6). Man's original position was lost because God exercised punishment. The Bible is a testimonial for God's discipline by both commandment and example. The Law (10 Commandments) came with a stiff penalty for violation. Some consequences that scream out at us from the Old Testament are: 1) Adam lost his home, his innocence, his son and his life; 2) Lot lost his home, his influence and his wife; 3) David lost his respect, a mighty warrior and a child. And this pattern is repeated in the New Testament and in these last days.

I was raised in the 1950's and 1960's in an era known for its use of LSD. I myself was an LSD baby, not like you are thinking; I grew up under the influence of "Leather Strap Discipline." Before I even knew that I had a fragile psyche or that my self-image could be damaged by my parent's invasion of my personal space. My parents had the audacity to use a leather strap (which alternatively held up my dad's pants) to rearrange my thinking or adjust my attitude. A "Time-out" was something that stopped play at a sporting event not a discipline tool. And now these many years later, there is a deprived generation grown up without the benefit of correction or discipline. Today it is common and almost expected that children rule the roost, displaying an unruly, egotistical and rebellious demeanor whose psyche is more twisted than mine. Everyone must finish in first place and be the first picked on the team and win or lose get a big trophy.

His Punishment is Deserving

To use the word punishment precludes that a crime has been committed and a guilty party identified. In a civilized society great care is taken to protect the innocent and bring the violator to justice. Our system of punishment has three objectives: 1) to satisfy justice, make amends, or restore personal property; 2) to rehabilitate the offender/criminal; 3) to detour others from traveling down a bad road. In a perfect world there would be no crime therefore there would be no need for punishment. In a fair world all the criminals would be caught, tried and punished and at the same time no innocent would ever be mistakenly convicted. However, our world is neither perfect or fair. Injustice may happen as frequently as justice. No doubt many of us have friends or family members that have been wrongfully accused and possibly convicted of crimes they did not commit. In our corrupt system there is no justice, the victim is publicly assaulted while the perpetrator enjoys great protection of his/her rights. The rich and/or the celebrity may be excused or punished with a slap on the wrist while the poor or unrepresented suffer tremendous consequences for their wrong. Recently in my local news, a woman was arrested and charged with cruelty to animals for leaving a dog inside the fence of an unmanned animal shelter. Yet the same system exonerates a woman that abandons her baby on the steps of a fire-station. I don't get it, apparently, I am no judge of the level or severity of crimes. I can't distinguish much difference between keeping a dog on a leash, keeping a goldfish in an aquarium, keeping a giraffe at the zoo or Shamu living in the pool palace at SeaWorld. Maybe my cynicism is why I can't understand the color television set and the expensive work out devices provided for inmates that have in my humble opinion forfeited the right to those luxuries. At best we are an imperfect people imposing imperfect laws intended to create some sense of sanity and order.

God on the other hand is perfect and His laws are both holy and just. God is not only the perfect lawgiver but also the perfect judge. An Old Testament queen traveled a great distance to be exposed to the brilliance and wisdom displayed in judgment by King Solomon; but there is a "greater than Solomon" in judgment and that is God. "God is no respecter of persons" (Acts 10:34). No uniform or pedigree will exempt you from justice before a holy God. Several scriptures reveal this quality or attribute of God. (See Deuteronomy 10:17-18; II Chronicles 19:7; Romans 2:11; Galatians 2:6; Ephesians 6:9; Colossians 3:25; and *I Peter 1:13-21).

During my formative years I may have received a whipping or two that I did not deserve but the balances were absolutely tipped in my favor because there were hundreds that were justified but not given. It is possible that I just wore my parents down. God is just and right, and I have deserved every stripe He ever laid. I want to go on record right here and right now that like Jeremiah I thank God for His mercy (Lamentations 3:21-23). We are foolish and wrong to assume that God winks at sin or that because we have gotten away with it so far that God really doesn't care. In the area of "punishment" I feel a kindred spirit with the repentant thief on the cross at Jesus' side. He said we are getting what we deserve (Luke 23:40-43) and upon acknowledging his sin and placing his faith in Jesus, he was forgiven and experienced the mercy of the LORD.

His Punishment is Discerning

God has a way of revealing the guilty transgressor, I don't pretend to understand all His ways. Isaiah said that His ways are higher than our ways and also past finding out. In Achan's case the revealing was filtering down through the tribe to the family to the man until Achan was left standing in front of Joshua (Joshua 7:14 – 20) Although thirty-six people died needlessly because of Achan's sin, the punishment of God fell on Achan and his family who were also culpable in his transgression. In Numbers 5:11 – 31 the case of the wondering woman was determined through the test of the bitter water. On other occasions it was through Urim and Thummin; anyway, God has always revealed the guilt of the guilty and crafted a particularized punishment appropriate to the offense. Although the sins of a nation shall be judged, it is the personal sins yielding personal consequences and exacting

God's personal attention that really increases our knowledge of God. As dealt with earlier it is the experiential knowledge of God's work that draws us close.

I can recall a few occasions in my childhood where I had the undivided attention of my mother or father. It was one of those one on one meeting of the minds. Usually, my mind was swayed in their direction. I got to know them better with each of those personal encounters. Now nearly 50 years removed from that last encounter I can without reservation say that "knowing them through punishment" has made me a much better man. In fact, I considered their discipline style to be so "spot-on" that I chose it over the Dr. Spock approach used by many of my peers.

God is a specialist in discipline and targets the time and place of His discipline for the greatest benefit. It has been my experience that God never swings a sledgehammer to set a thumbtack; but God is capable of precision with the sledgehammer if it becomes the tool that is required. He is long-suffering and merciful but has never lowered the bar on holiness.

My mom went with me on my first day of school. I cried when she left me there. It is a little embarrassing now in retrospect. In subsequent years, grades 2 – 6 instead of accompanying me to school on day one she sent me with a note for my teachers. It read,

> "Dear teacher,
>
> You have my permission to discipline Edwin Dean however you feel would be appropriate. Please do not hesitate to call on me for any reason and most especially if he becomes a discipline problem.
>
> Thank you, Alice Button

Some of those letters never arrived at their intended destination. One day my 5th grade teacher at Mae M. Walters elementary school decided to keep the entire class after school for thirty minutes because she couldn't determine the guilty party of a 5th degree misdemeanor. My teacher's actions warranted another note from my mom.

"Dear teacher,

I have given you permission to discipline my son by detaining him after school, by making him clean the chalkboard, by making him sit in the corner with a dunce cap on his head or by paddling him for any wrong doing that he has done. But I have no intention of allowing him to be disciplined for something he hasn't done. Please release him from your custody when the school day has ended.

Thank you, Alice Button

(That note was delivered)

The Bible declares regarding chastening that, "God dealeth with you as with sons" (Hebrews 12:7). Effective chastening is always rendered to its beneficiary with an explanation for the need of it. The wrongdoing is identified, and the appropriate punishment administered. God works that way so that the recipient of the discipline doesn't have to wonder about the "why." Sometimes discipline comes because we hesitate or don't respond quickly enough. (Growing up I always had to the count of three) Sometimes it comes because we choose to go the wrong way. (Jonah comes to mind) I have been whipped for both. Either way it demonstrates that God's punishment is not arbitrary.

His Punishment is Disturbing

If there is, and there is, rejoicing in heaven over one sinner that repenteth (Matthew 15:7) then the flip side of that coin may also be true. That there is sorrow over the lack of repentance from the masses or even the one. The Bible often declares the long-suffering nature of God and that He is not willing that any should perish. That is a difficult concept for my finite mind to fathom. I have a sadistic side. One of my favorite sounds can be heard just after sunset from my front porch; the sound of mosquitoes casually and innocently flying into my bug zapper. That is just one of my many flaws that keeps me grounded. God finds no pleasure in the death of the wicked (Ezekiel 33:11). I have not discovered everything that can be discovered about God; indeed, I will be learning about Him for eternity. What I have learned about God and His discipline is that it breaks His heart to discipline His children. I can't imagine that I am the only one that heard the phrase "This is going to hurt me more than it hurts you", but I did hear it almost daily. I genuinely thought that my mom must not be doing it right because I was pretty sure that I was getting the worst end of the deal. Then I grew up and understood the pain of parenting and the responsibility of breaking the will of a rebellious child traveling down a bad path. My heavenly father set the benchmark of discipline so high that I cannot attain it. In the motive and spirit of discipline He is perfect. It is His love that drives Him to discipline. I have come to know Him experientially in the "Wonder of Salvation", the "Work Shop" and the "Wood Shed" (way too often) and someday soon I will know Him at the "Wedding Supper."

Jesus, the victim of hostility and rejection, displays the greatest of character when instead of torching Jerusalem for their disdain for Him, He wept over them instead. He knew there were thousands there for whom He would die that never would believe on Him. The love of God is so pure that it is exclusive by nature. God's love for me means that He hates everything that potentially hurts me. I hate congestive heart failure; it snuffed the life out of my earthly father. Likewise, I hate dementia because it slowly tore my mom away from me. The love that God has for His children will not allow Him to be idle and watch potential harm find lodging and/or take up residence within us on His watch. Nothing about this great love of Christ prohibits us from exercising our free will to live in rebellion or to backslide out of His favor. But He loves you too much to let you stay there without correction. The writer of Hebrews confirms this principle in chapter twelve verses five through eleven. God's purpose in punishment is not to inflict pain but to awaken the child of God to the dangers of rebellion and draw them back into fellowship. His holiness demands that punishment will come but

His love and mercy exhibit patience and long-suffering. There is no scripture to suggest that punishment has no impact on God; but contrariwise many scriptures reveal that He is moved by the infirmities we face and even the choices we make.

Up until now I have been focusing on God's punishment exacted upon His children. It has come time to shift gears and widen the scope of this truth. All sin will be punished. "The soul that sinneth it shall die." (Ezekiel 18:20a). "It is appointed unto men once to die, but after this the judgment..." (Hebrews 9:27). "For God shall bring every work into judgment, with every secret thing, whether it be good or whether it be evil." (Ecclesiastes 12:14) Eventually every knee will bow, and every tongue will confess that Jesus Christ is Lord. Something from this scene leads me to believe that we will all acknowledge that He is just and holy. His judgment is true, and His punishment is just (Romans 14:10). The mercies of God will not be available on the day of judgment. The holiness of God and the love of God walked together with man in the garden of Eden. Man's sin drove a wedge between these two divine attributes of God. That wedge existed for over 4000 years until they met together again just outside the walled city of Jerusalem in a place called in Latin "Calvary" or for the locals "Golgotha" (the place of the skull). The holiness of God could look again on man through the redemptive work and the shed blood of the spotless Lamb of God, Jesus Christ. If you are counting on some future demonstration of God's redemptive work, you will be sadly and eternally disappointed come judgment day. Any future act of God that ignores your sin and rejection of His son Jesus would put Christ and His violent death to an open mockery. God spared not the angels that transgressed, He spared not Noah's world, He spared not Sodom, He spared not His Son, and He will not spare you. Except ye repent ye shall all likewise perish.

"This is going to hurt me more than it hurts you."

If I have mistakenly presented God as one anxious to destroy, juggling fire and brimstone looking for a place to consume then my apologies to you and to God for I know God better than that. But please don't make the mistake of indifference towards God's invitation, there will be a last one. Sinner, repent and turn to Christ, He is eager to forgive and cleanse you from all unrighteousness. Wanderer, repent and return to Christ, He is waiting and anxious for the return of His prodigal son. God is love and one of the most loving things He does is to correct us lest we stray and become the meal for the wolf. I will leave you with a portion of scripture that well reflects the chastening work of the Lord.

> *"For the Lord will not cast off forever: But though he cause grief, yet will he have compassion according to the multitude of his mercies. For he doth not afflict willingly nor grieve the children of men. To crush under his feet all the prisoners of the earth, To turn aside the right of a man before the face of the most High, To subvert a man in his cause, the Lord approveth not. Who is he that saith, and it cometh to pass, when the Lord commandeth it not? Out of the mouth of the most High proceedeth not evil and good? Wherefore doth a living man complain, a man for the punishment of his sins? Let us search and try our ways, and turn again to the Lord. Let us lift up our heart with our hands unto God in the heavens. We have transgressed and have rebelled: thou hast not pardoned."* (Lamentations 3:31-42)

My Prayer: My Gracious and Merciful Heavenly Father, I thank You that You have not chastened as I have deserved but have been long-suffering. I confess my sin and acknowledge my weakness. I am prone to wander outside of Your will. I pray that day by day you will give me wisdom over the lures of the devil and a passion to please You. Father, when it becomes necessary to chasten me, help me to quickly repent and learn to obey. Help me not resent your compassion even when it is meted out in discipline. In Jesus name, Amen.

Chapter Seven
KNOWING HIM IN HIS PURITY

I Peter 1:15-16 "But as He which hath called you is holy, so be ye holy in all manner of conversation; Because it is written, Be ye holy; for I am holy."

The year was 1879, James Gamble and Harley Proctor began marketing their new floating soap. The name for their silky white soap was inspired by a Sunday Morning message from Psalm 45:8. Its iconic name is mirrored by its iconic slogan; the soap, "Ivory" and that slogan (Ninety-nine and 44/100% pure) have survived one-hundred and forty years. I have always wondered what the remaining 0.56% ingredients were. Apparently, I lived a boring childhood. When it comes to purity God sets a higher standard than Proctor & Gamble. With God there is an unmarred, untainted and unpolluted 100% pureness. His essence is without flaw and is always in every circumstance only Holy. Admittedly He is the only one that has ever been able to make such a claim. Yet the bar is raised for every Christian to pursue. When the Apostle Paul penned his letter to the saints in Rome, he acknowledged our sin by nature and practice, but he also challenged us to live no longer therein. (Romans 6:2) There is an expectation that we would pursue holiness and yield not to sin. Conquering sin is the on-going work of God's Spirit in us called sanctification. This great work is accomplished through God's pruning and man's purging. (See John 15:2 & II Timothy 2:21) This work of Christ is an inside out work. When the heart is made right then the body in subjection will follow. This is a lesson that the superficial Pharisees never learned. They were whited sepulchers externally but inside full of dead men's bones. (Matthew 23:27) If putting on a white garment and smelling perfumed up could make one pure then the Pharisees would be our model. But Christ pronounced woe on them and called them hypocrites. When sin becomes so exceedingly sinful that we are repulsed by it and we desire to shed it like a dead snake skin, then Godly sorrow has led us to repentance, and we are a candidate for the Master's surgical skills that can carve away the cancer of sin. (Romans 7:13) This work of the Master crafting us into Christlikeness is not a comfortable work. Sometimes He uses divine tools like the Bible, the Holy Spirit or the refiner's fire to remove the impurities, and sometimes he uses potsherds (other people) to scrape away our less than Christlike character. But either way His intention is always the same: to conform us to the image of His Son. (Romans 8:29 & 12:1-2) The Apostle Peter put it like this, "…Be ye holy; for I am holy." (I Peter 1:15-16) God forbid that we should ever be content in our sinning or abandon our pursuit of righteousness.

The word "pure" is used 97 times in the Bible and is used to modify a myriad of objects i.e. (gold, myrrh, incense, doctrine, wool, offering, water, conscience and religion etc.) and it is always used to identify something without contaminates or impurities. That is without a doubt true concerning the Lord Jesus Christ. When Isaiah saw the LORD in the year that King Uzziah died, he heard the angelic heralds announce Him as "Holy, holy, holy" (Isaiah 6:3) and almost simultaneously he identified himself as "undone" and "unclean" (6:5). There is not an area where the LORD could improve. There are at least three benefits to Knowing Christ in His Purity. I should like to consider them and be brought closer to His likeness by being exposed to His purity.

His Purity Provides a Sharp Contrast to our Sin

He is in every way perfect and pure. It is His purity that has been set as the bar by which we shall all be judged. When a man sets his focus on Christ, then Christ' light exposes man's imperfections and flaws. If we choose to remain in the dark, our tarnished lives may be less visible, and we might pretend that they don't exist but deceiving ourselves doesn't remove the stain. "But if we will walk in the light as He is in the light, we have fellowship one with another, and the blood of Jesus Christ His Son cleanseth us from all sin." (I John 1:7) If we will look unto Jesus, we will get an unbiased glimpse into our own filthy rags. In much the same way as the law was given to show us our sin (Romans 3:19-20), Christ' holiness is revealed to expose to us our sin. If we compare ourselves alongside of others, then as long as our neighbors are lawless, lying, lazy and lethargic we look pretty good. After all, as long as you are faster than the slowest man in the forest then you don't have to worry about the bear; or might there be more than one bear. We tend to use that comparative mentality for tall, short, pretty, strong or even fat. So long as there is someone worse, undoubtedly, we are okay. Unfortunately, that is not how it will look on judgment day. Someone once said, God doesn't grade on the curve. He grades on the cross.

Many years ago, I was coming home from a hospital visit in Lakeland, Florida and I was traveling down a long stretch of road through the Green Swamp (Hwy 471) and I was exceeding the speed limit. I was doing 65 in a 55 when suddenly someone I recognized blew by me like I was sitting still. It was on. Well as it turns out I couldn't catch him; but one of Florida Highway Patrol's finest did. I remember that as I drove by him on the side of the road, I was thinking, it serves him right. In just about one minute I discovered that there was more than one Highway Patrolman on that desolate stretch of road. He was not sympathetic at all that my friend was driving faster than me. The law was 55 MPH. Making Jesus your standard can/will have an impact for righteousness's sake. I'm confident that the Apostle John had insight to this truth that I do not have, but I have found a verse God gave to him to be very intriguing. In First John chapter three and verse two John wrote: "Beloved, now are we the sons of God, and it doth not yet appear what we shall be: but we know that, when He shall appear, we shall be like Him; for we shall see Him as He is." What a rich verse. I know that it is true for the eternal ages, that we shall have sinless existence and be completely perfect in our glorified bodies; but what if seeing Him as He is could be applied to our mortal existence. To the degree that we can see Him, our lives are transformed toward righteousness. The Psalmist, David, sheds light to this truth in Psalm 17:15, "As for me, I will behold thy face in righteousness: I shall be satisfied, when I awake, with Thy likeness."

We tend to excuse our sin and think that because everybody is doing it, that God will just shrug His shoulders. Maybe if we say, "God understands" or "I'm only human", then the consequences of our sin will be reduced. Better yet, we can negotiate with God; "I will sing in the choir if you will let me… ___(fill in the blank)___. Holiness is not negotiable, and God is not in the bargaining business. When we set our sights on things above (Colossians 3:2) then we can hone in on our LORD's purity and if we look closely enough, we can see the disappointment in His face when we sin.

His Purity Pierces with Strong Conviction

It is not enough that we recognize God's purity if we manage to be untouched and unchanged by that encounter. Every child of God has the eternal presence of the Holy Spirit of God living within them. That is a promise that Jesus gave us and the message that Paul delivered to the saints at Rome in Romans 8:9 "But ye are not in the flesh, but in the Spirit, if so be that the Spirit of God dwell in you. Now if any man have not the Spirit of Christ, he is none of His." In fact, chapters seven and eight are all about the struggle and war that exists between the flesh and the Spirit. Every child of God has the capacity to resist the Devil and have victory over sin. John shares truth about this struggle in the epistle of First John, chapters 1 – 3. He is not preaching "Sinless Perfection" but "Sinless Pursuit." Flip Wilson may have you convinced that the devil made you do it, but not so according to the Word of God. Sin can be easily defined as doing or saying or going where Jesus would not. And, the flip side of that equation is likewise true, not doing or saying or going where Jesus would is sin. Jesus did nothing that brought displeasure to His Father and He did everything

He was sent to do. So much so that He could say, "it is finished" the entire assignment, the will of the Father and the example for mankind.

My personal experience has been that conviction is not sweet, in fact it is quite bitter, but if it accomplishes its desired end, it will yield peaceable fruits of righteousness. It is the goodness of God that leadeth thee to repentance. (See Romans 2:4 and Hebrews 12:11) If you have experienced and know the alarming conviction of the Holy Spirit then it is a good sign that you are a child of God. It is possible however to be a child of God and not sense His conviction. Two scenarios come to mind: First, you may have seared your conscience with a hot iron desensitizing yourself to God's wooing; and Second, God may have already turned you over to the devil for the destruction of the flesh. (See I Timothy 4:2 and I Corinthians 5:5) During Jesus' ministry a group of scribes and Pharisees brought a woman before Him that was guilty of adultery; Jesus only stooped and wrote in the ground and then challenged the jurors to pass judgment after self-examination. The woman's accusers were convicted and left her alone with Jesus. I can't comprehend what He wrote but His knowledge of their sins and His challenge that only the guiltless cast stones would easily have sparked this conviction. (See John 8:1-11)

> *"Every child of God has the capacity to resist the Devil and have victory over sin."*

I have been privileged to visit Israel 24 times and one of my favorite sites is the house of Caiaphas the high priest. The scene provides the backdrop for the mock trial of Jesus, the denial of Peter and the convicting message from the rooster. But there is one more mentionable event on that stage, when the cock crew, "the Lord turned, and looked upon Peter. And Peter remembered the word of the Lord." In view of that gaze from the spotless Lamb of God, "Peter went out and wept bitterly." That is exactly what the piercing, strong conviction of Christ in His purity looks like. (See Luke 22:60-62)

His Purity Promotes a Sincere Contract

So how do we move from Holy Spirit conviction to victory over sin? This might be the hub question of Christianity. Every pastor has experienced the responding penitent sinner coming down the aisle to re-dedicate their life to Christ, only to watch them wander away with little or no change from their conviction. They may have expected a bolt of lightning or some heavenly confirmation to their sincerity but that didn't happen, and they returned to their mire. In First Corinthians chapter six, Paul challenges this carnal audience with the fact that our "bodies are the members of Christ" (6:15) and that our bodies are "the temple of the Holy Ghost..." This reality demands of us that we keep our body in subjection. I have found that making a contract with the members of my body has hedged me into a more circumspect walk and protected me from wandering. Have I arrived? No, a thousand times over, but I find myself pressing harder toward the mark and rejoicing in each victory. Since temptation is common to man and woman, I can share my weaknesses with confidence that there are others in my boat. There are four clauses to my contract; feel free to add more.

My eyes. I will join the Psalmist in saying, "I will set no wicked thing before mine eyes:" (Psalm 101:3) William Shakespeare said, "The eyes are the window to your soul." No one is strong enough to overcome the influence of looking upon what we shouldn't. Jeremiah penned this truth in Lamentations 3:51, "Mine eye affecteth mine heart because of all the daughters of my city." Jesus said if your eye offends you pluck it out, (Matthew 18:9) don't let your eye destroy you. This is one of the devil's greatest resources and his primary gateway into our minds. The billboards, television, fashion and now the internet pose an attack against my desire to protect my eyes from evil. David's wandering eyes cost him dearly and was one of the greatest kinks in his armor.

My feet. There are seven abominable things to the LORD and one of the things that made the list is, "feet that be swift running to mischief." (Proverbs 6:19) Whether you are running to engage in mischief or just to observe, the LORD hates it. There is a message here for the mobs that are playing havoc on society today. God pronounced a blessing for those who will honor him with their feet. Psalm 1:1 reads, "Blessed is the man that <u>walketh</u> not in the counsel of the ungodly, nor <u>standeth</u> in the way of sinners..."

My mouth. In our kitchen hangs a plaque from Cracker Barrell that serves as a constant reminder to my struggles with this clause: "Lord please put your arm around my shoulder and your hand over my mouth." I encounter people every day with "foot in mouth" disease. Many of us rev-up our mouths before putting our minds in gear. This is an especially fatal trait for a child of God, as it ruins our testimony and opportunity to share Christ with others. "Pardon my French" doesn't erase the damage done by our vulgar speech. James devotes an entire chapter of his book to this subject. In James 3:10-11 he declares, "Out of the same mouth proceedeth blessing and cursing. My brethren, these things ought not so to be. Doth a fountain send forth at the same place sweet water and bitter?" The implied answer is, NO!

My hands. I am reminded regularly about washing my hands and in the days of this pandemic it is presumed to be the major defense against contamination. The first element of this clause involves "clean hands." (See James 4:8) Touch not the unclean thing. The second element involves "hard-working hands." (See Ecclesiastes 9:10) Whatever we put our hands to, it should be done with our might and as unto the LORD. In many ways my mom was a Proverbs 31 woman, but most especially with her hands. "Idle hands are the devil's workshop." Mom's hands were not idle, and they were always at work for others. (See Proverbs 31:19-20) She could outwork most men even when she was 82 years old. She raked five acres of leaves four times a year. The last element in this clause concerns holding on to the plow until God calls me home. Faithfully serving and worshiping; lifting holy hands to Him who is worthy of all our praise.

An old song comes to mind: "Born to Serve the Lord." One verse helps me with this contract: "My hands were made to help my neighbor, My eyes were made to read God's word, My feet were made to walk in His footsteps, My body is the temple of the LORD"

My Prayer: My Father in heaven, hallowed is Your name, You are holy, Your name and all Your works are holy and pure. Your holiness has exposed my sinfulness. I am praying that right now my sin might be as exceedingly sinful in my sight as it is in Yours. May my earnest desire be to be found in the likeness of Your precious Son, Jesus, in whose name I pray. Amen.

Chapter Eight
KNOWING HIM IN HIS POWER

Philippians 3:10 "That I may know Him, and the power of His resurrection…"

According to a report from the International Health, Racquet and Sportsclub Association dated May of 2019, (no I don't subscribe) the United States citizenry spends over 32 billion dollars annually on memberships to fitness establishments. If you add the monies spent on food supplements and body building equipment, that 32 billion increases exponentially. A few years ago, a nationally recognized fitness chain opened a location near my home. With an interest in losing some weight, toning up and reducing my overall body fat, I joined. I kept meticulous records and at the end of just one year I had lost almost six hundred dollars. A common denominator among neighborhood garage or yard sales is the barely used treadmill or the never used elliptical machine. Hell, and the emergency room have at least this one thing in common: they are both full of people with good intentions.

Several Bible characters displayed an unusual power of a divine nature. First to my mind is Samson, an Old Testament judge, that took out thousands of Philistines. What really intrigues me about Samson is that the source of his strength was what everyone wanted to discover; or maybe more accurately it was the search for his kryptonite that society sought. He may have had a strikingly chiseled body, but it wasn't his great exercise regiment, or his strict diet that set him apart from others or it would have been discovered and imitated. Delilah and the Philistines were in pursuit of his secret in order to unplug his power source. David is worth an honorable mention in the strength department also. Before he took down the giant, he had already killed a lion and a bear. And apparently, he took one of his father's sheep out of the lion's mouth before he killed it. (See I Samuel 17:32-36) That is not on my bucket list. The Bible records many of David's victories in battle. It was his great accomplishments that caused Saul's heart to be filled with jealousy. The women in Israel were singing songs of David's victories more so than Saul's, even ten-fold. There are also the mighty men that served as David's military secret service. Their accomplishments are enumerated in First Chronicles chapters eleven and twelve. You wouldn't want to run in to any one of these men in the heat of battle.

Much like physical strength, divine power comes at a great price, but it can't be bought. In Acts 8:19, during the incredible outpouring of God's Spirit, Simon, a new convert, thought that he might be able to write a check and "shazam" he could wield around the same power as Philip, Peter and John. But Simon was scolded by Peter and instructed to pray for forgiveness. Just before sending the twelve apostles out on mission, Jesus "gave them power..." (Matthew 10:1) Divine power is certainly obtainable. It may look different in the 21st century but it can still move mountains and defeat the enemy. The Apostle Paul warned Timothy that in the last days there would come a form of godliness that denies the power that should accompany it. (II Timothy 3:5) The preceding list of abominable sins (verses 1-4) that identify this group are trademarks of right here and right now. God does reward faithful, obedient, selfless servants with unusual and sometimes invisible power of a divine sort. However, nowhere in scripture is it indicated that you can recite some magic rhyme or wave a magic wand and display this power. In fact, the opposite is true. God provides uncanny strength to those who are on the battlefield and have come to the end of themselves, when no resources are visible. God loves to defy the odds. He has always used the small, the remnant, the weak, the outnumbered, the outsized so that He can receive the glory that He alone is worthy. Paul declared that, "...not many wise men after the flesh, not many mighty, not many noble, are called:" (I Corinthians 1:26) For God to give this divine power to the unprepared and/or the insubordinate would be about the same as giving a bazooka to an infant. But when we are in complete surrender to Him and the enemy is gloating about their coming victory, then God shows up and shows out.

This great desire "to know Him and the power of His resurrection" that Paul had is an honorable desire. I can't think of anyone off hand that wouldn't want that kind of power. But how can I have it? Or can I have it? God would never commission you to a task and not equip you or empower you for that task. It may take the rigorous discipline of boot camp or the experience of standing alone in the day of battle, but God's power is still available. A power of this magnitude must have some secret ingredient. Indeed, some of the most powerful Christians I have ever known have come in frail packages, not very intimidating in stature, but mighty in the hands of God. I do have some Christian friends that have God's power resting on them but the two people that I wanted praying for me were my mom and a dear elderly lady named Bessie Turner. They had a connection with God that I rarely see, they didn't have halos hovering over their heads, but it was obvious that they knew God and God knew them. They had His power. Let's consider some keys to this great power and what might be considered the price you must pay to enjoy "Knowing Him in His Power."

The Price of Humility Before Him

The elusive quality of humility has been identified as so fragile that the moment you think you have grasped it, it is gone. As mentioned earlier, God is not looking for the mighty to bow-up and be noticed for their spiritual physique. But for the meek and lowly who stand only by His strength. Humility in the face of your peers may be a difficult assignment because quite honestly, they put their pants on one leg at a time too. But the challenge of humility in the sight of the LORD should be easy. James records this message to his first century audience,

"Humble yourselves in the sight of the Lord, and He shall lift you up. (James 4:10) And a few verses earlier he stated that, "God resisteth the proud but giveth grace unto the humble." (Verse 6) This attribute may not have accompanied Samson, but it certainly applies to King David, who the Bible says was a man after God's own heart. That being true, Jesus was indeed a humble man though He was God. To the Philippian Church Paul wrote, "Let this mind be in you which was also in Christ Jesus: Who being in the form of God, thought it not robbery to be equal with God: But made Himself of no reputation, and took upon Him the form of a servant, and was made in the likeness of men: And being found in the fashion as a man, He humbled Himself, and became obedient unto death, even the death of the cross. Wherefore God also hath highly exalted Him, and given Him a name which is above every name:." (Philippians 2:5-9) Pride and humility cannot co-exist; they are mutually exclusive. Of the seven abominations to the LORD, [(cardinal sins) not my terminology] the first mentioned by Solomon is "A proud look…" (Proverbs 6:17) And it makes sense because pride and a haughty spirit are a recipe for destruction and a fall. (See Proverbs 16:18) Among God's requirements for man is "…to walk humbly with thy God." (Micah 6:8)

The Apostle Paul often shared his weakness and/or his infirmities. II Corinthians chapter twelve is a testimony of Paul's humility as he exposes his weakness. Paul speaks of his weakness at least a half dozen times (I Cor. 2:3, I Cor. 4:10, II Cor. 11:29, 12:9, 12:10, 13:4 & 13:9) He said, "though I be nothing" (II Corinthians 12:11) and no doubt believed that. When I think of Paul I think of a frail, crippled, blind old man but don't let that lull you into thinking that he could be easily defeated. Many tried to kill him but God's power prevailed time and time again. Very few have ever risen to the stature of this giant of the cause of Christ, and yet he said, "That I may know Him, and the power of His resurrection…." There is this power that is greater than death. Death may be a formidable foe, but it has been and will be finally defeated as man's last enemy. This victory comes through resurrection power. Christians have this power at their disposal because we that were dead are made alive in Christ and enjoy this eternal life that has conquered death.

The Price of Hunger for Him

It is the pursuit of Christ that brings resurrection power; it is not the pursuit of power that delivers it. Paul had a hunger for Christ that was never completely satisfied until his race down here was over. But he was determined to run his race; and pursue his course; and fight the good fight of faith; and press toward the mark until he stood before his LORD in judgment. Power is what the LORD gave him because of the drive and hunger he had for Christ. Paul worked on this passion of knowing the LORD in power like an athlete in training, it affected every area of his life. He made huge sacrifice for it. Paul was a man on a path for greatness according to this world's scale. He was a ranking member of society, well-schooled, a Roman citizen, a pedigree among the Jewish nation; yet he said, "But what things were gain to me, those I counted loss for Christ. Yea doubtless and I count all things but loss for the excellency of the knowledge of Christ Jesus my Lord: for whom I have suffered the loss of all things, and do count them but dung, that I may win Christ." (Philippians 3:7-8)

I am prone to treating Christ like the flavor of the month or someone I need for a certain season or situation. Paul made this a daily ambition and would not waiver in his commitment or pursuit of Christ. Knowing Christ is the spring of living water, the well that will not go dry, the barrel of meal that shall not waste or the cruse of oil that never fails. Many accounts are provided of mere men and women that experienced this level of sustaining from God; not because they sought power or fame, but because in humility and great hunger they sought the LORD. Consider this prescription for power found in I Corinthians 2:1-5.

> *"And I brethren, when I came to you, came not with excellency of speech or of wisdom, declaring unto you the testimony of God. For I determined not to know any thing among you, save Jesus Christ, and Him crucified.*

And I was with you in weakness, and in fear, and in much trembling. And my speech and my preaching was not with enticing words of man's wisdom, but in demonstration of the Spirit and of power: That your faith should not stand in the wisdom of men, but in the power of God."

The Price of Honor to Him

Admittedly there is a close connection between the previously mentioned humility and the thoughts of this section. Humility does honor the LORD and giving honor to the LORD is evidence of humility. They serve as bookends to this divine power; they prop it up from either side. They are the cause and effect of His power resting upon you. God does not provide this gift of power so that you can consume it upon your own lusts, but rather that it may be used to point others to Christ. Flaunting your humility is not attractive and it does not exalt Christ. Likewise, desiring credit, attention, praise or recognition is an insult to God. He alone is worthy of praise. If it is His power on loan to you, then honor Him with the victory. Proclaim it aloud, let the whole world know "that power belongeth unto God." (Psalm 62:11) Of necessity the Apostle Paul mentioned his infirmities and weakness. He did say he would boast of them, but he qualifies this statement by sharing that Christ may be seen and that he could experience the power of God. As an instructor to the Corinthian saints, he shared his life's story and the lessons he had received of the LORD. In life or in death he was yielded to God's purpose and pleasure. In infirmities, reproaches, necessities, persecutions and distresses he trusted God. (See II Corinthians 12:10) He claimed that he was ready to be offered, and that he would gladly spend or be spent for Christ and/or His causes.

God can and will still move Sycamore trees and mountains either figuratively or literally. The problem is our confidence in God and our own connection to God as a source of power. The Apostle Paul said, "I can do all things through Christ which strengtheneth me." (Philippians 4:13) He was willing to put God on the spot with the impossible. Malachi gave us God's message about proving Him and seeing that He would pour out blessings. The Bible promises that He "is able to do exceeding abundantly above what we ask or think, according to the power that worketh in us." (Ephesians 3:20) We pray shallow prayers and ask insignificant things because we have so little faith. Or, maybe it is because we want to spare God the embarrassment of failure. We ask for only what we believe we can accomplish without His assistance. What great things are you asking God for? What have you prayed for that only God through divine power could do? Shame on me and shame on you for presenting such an impotent God to the world. As a child I discovered this truth. "God can do anything, anything, God can do anything but fail." The early church witnessed God's power routinely and as a result grew exponentially. This modern generation needs a shot of biblical "Geritol" to energize our confidence in God and to experience His power. While reading through the book of Acts, the impossible happens on every page. One such message is delivered in Acts chapter four. Notice an excerpt from this story.

> Acts 4: 7-10 "And when they had set them in the midst, they asked, By what power, or by what name, have ye done this? Then Peter, filled with the Holy Ghost, said unto them, Ye rulers of the people, and elders of Israel, If we this day be examined of the good deed done to the impotent man, by what means he is made whole; Be it known unto you all, and to all the people of Israel, that by the name of Jesus Christ of Nazareth, who ye crucified, whom God raised from the dead, even by Him doth this man stand here before you whole."

> "This modern generation needs a shot of biblical 'Geritol' to energize our confidence in God and to experience His power."

I have been fascinated by eagles most of my life and have quite a collection of wood carved eagles. My fascination is with their strength, their talons, their eyesight, their wingspan, well everything about them. They are the symbol of our nation because of their power. An eagle soars through the sky while the hummingbird barely lifts to the treetops. The hummingbird flaps its wings as much as 200 times a second whereas the eagle scarcely more than two times a second. Yet the eagle climbs to great heights, why? Because of their enormous power and ability to utilize the wind. May God grant us the wherewithal to ride the winds of the Holy Spirit and soar in His power.

My prayer: Heavenly Father, I bow before you, I am a frail, weak dependent child. I pray that you will grant power for each assignment, as much as I can be trusted with. I pray that you will receive all the honor and that for every victory you give, I will recognize your hand and give you the praise, credit and all glory. In Jesus name, Amen.

Chapter Nine
KNOWING HIM IN HIS PAIN

> *"That I may know Him, and the power of His resurrection, and the fellowship of His sufferings, being made conformable unto His death;"* (Philippians 3:10)

> *"For even hereunto were ye called: because Christ also suffered for us, leaving us an example, that ye should follow His steps:"* (I Peter 2:21)

God presented the opportunity for me to serve as a bereavement counselor with a hospice group twelve years ago and I have enjoyed offering hope to those who have suffered such great loss. With this experience I have gained insight into the language and terminology associated with end-of-life care. There are documents available to patients as they face death that provide instruction as to the care and treatment they desire. These documents are legally necessary to ensure that one's wishes are honored in the event they lose the ability to communicate them for themselves. Possible choices include: a living will, a medical surrogate or even a "my 5 wishes" contract. All of these documents and/or appointments reveal patient's rights to be honored and protected that generally include terminology like: Do not Resuscitate, no heroic measures, no artificial life support, fed by natural means only and keep me clean and free of pain. No one wants to pass from this life while agonizing in pain. In fact, I, don't know anyone that wants to live in pain either. Pain management is a big industry. It includes: surgery, TENS units, pharmaceuticals (Darvocet, Percocet, hydro-codeine, morphine, Novocain, Tylenol 3, Aleve, Bufferin, Tramadol, Ibuprofen, Fentanyl, alcohol and dozens more) and even hypnosis. Whatever it takes to achieve our pain-free goal. One might argue that as we desensitize ourselves from pain, we also make joy and happiness harder to experience.

If pain-free is our goal, what then would cause Paul and Peter to pursue and even embrace pain and suffering? Who in his right mind would sign-up for such a journey? I am well aware that many who have eagerly accompanied me in this pursuit to "Know Him" will want to get off the train at this stop. But, for those that stay aboard, the pleasure is worth the pain. Most of us have become so spoiled that we don't even tolerate inconvenience well much less pain. A preacher friend of mine, David Butts, was raised by a tough man, a farrier (horse-shoe-r) and he would not stand for one of his sons being fragile. He regularly asked his boys, "Can't you stand pain?" The correct and expected answer was "Yes Sir!"

At least three recent political figures have said, "I feel your pain." (Pat Buchanan, George Bush and Bill Clinton) They leave from their stage and go to their limousine for a ride back to their mansion to enjoy a seven-course meal prepared by the finest chefs. I am not convinced that they feel my pain. Jesus on the other hand, did submit to my sorrow, my suffering and my shame. He bore my cross, wore my crown of thorns, took my whipping and died my death. (See Hebrews 4:15 and Isaiah 53:3-10) In 1895, Mary T. Lothrap wrote a poem that would later be remembered by one line, "Walk a mile in his moccasins." She was challenging our prejudice and lack of empathy. Unless we know where they have been and what they have faced we cannot know why they have done what they did. I repeat, Jesus has experienced our pain; now He invites us to experience His pain. Will it hurt? Most assuredly. Although "weeping may endure for a night, ...joy cometh in the morning." (Psalm 30:5) Jesus endured His suffering (actually mine) by looking at the joy set before Him. (See Hebrews 12:2)

> "Christ mapped out the right course, giving us an example that we should follow His steps."

The truth about pain is that it is promised to all who will live Godly. (II Timothy 3:12) But, beyond the pain, happiness is also promised. Jesus said, "Blessed are they which are persecuted for righteousness' sake: for theirs is the kingdom of heaven. Blessed are ye, when men shall revile you, and persecute you, and shall say all manner of evil against you falsely, for my sake. Rejoice, and be exceeding glad: for great is your reward in heaven: for so persecuted they the prophets which were before you." (Matthew 5:10-12) The Apostle Peter said, "Happy are ye" (I Peter 3:14) while suffering for righteousness sake. Painlessness is not synonymous with happiness. Enjoying the power of Christ (see chapter seven) very likely hinges on joining Him in His pain. "No Pain - No Gain." Accepting the assignment of pain and continuing in this journey should be made possible and even easier when we consider these three great concepts:

The Model for This Pain

Not every pain deserves to be modeled i.e.: the pain of a criminal facing his punishment, the self-inflicted pain of sin or the "needless pain we bare" because we do not take our burdens to God in prayer. The pain that Christ suffered was inflicted on Him from many fronts. **First**, was **"The Pain of Sin."** Not His sin but ours. It could be that the most excruciating pain that our Lord endured was when the weight, the burden, the guilt of all humanity was placed on His shoulders at Calvary. So painful, so intense and so severe it was that the sun refused to shine, and His Father turned His face away. Despite the severity of this pain He was willing to drink this bitter cup and endure its pain. The Apostle Paul showed a similar willingness to endure this pain and claimed, "For I could wish that myself were accursed from Christ for my brethren, my kinsmen according to the flesh." (Romans 9:3) Christ suffered for sin that His suffering might give life to others. After the fall of man in the Garden of Eden, the LORD stated the consequences of sin upon man and woman. For woman, the LORD said, "I will greatly multiply thy sorrow and thy conception; in sorrow thou shalt bring forth children..." (Genesis 3:16) and Paul reminded Timothy of this truth in First Timothy chapter two and verse fifteen. Women endure this pain so that others can live. Once life has been delivered, the pain is soon forgotten. (See John 16:21 & Hebrews 12:2) If Christ is our model, then it is possible that we may suffer for the sins of others.

Second, was *"The Pain of Separation."* Jesus was well acquainted with this pain. Jesus was separated from and even hated by organized religion. Those that should have recognized Him and honored Him despised Him instead. The Jewish people by and large separated from Him. He came unto them, but they would not receive Him. (See John 1:11) Once Jesus did begin to amass a crowd, His preaching was so hard and the price so high that the crowds disbursed making a quick exit. (See John 6:66) He was not demanding a payment to obtain salvation, but warning that true disciples were going to pay a dear price for identifying with Him. Christ' separation is further identified and more severely displayed while on the cross when He cried out, "My God, My God, why hast Thou forsaken Me?" (Matthew 27:46) Even though there were men dying on either side of Jesus, for His cause, He died alone, separated from Heaven and Earth on a cross. Many Christians have faced a lesser level of separation. Their families have disowned them, they have been imprisoned or isolated not by their own choosing but only because of their faith. Jesus prepared us for this separation when He stated, "If any man come to me, and hate not his father, and mother, and wife, and children, and brethren, and sisters, yea, and his own life also, he cannot be my disciple." (Luke 14:26) Jesus has a right to call us out into separation, and He specifically did in II Corinthians 6:17 "Wherefore come out from among them, and be ye separate, saith the Lord, and touch not the unclean thing; and I will receive you." Jesus prayed for his followers just before His arrest and that prayer is recorded in John chapter seventeen. A careful look into this prayer reveals that Jesus knew the world would not be a perfect fit for His followers; nevertheless, He did not pray for our seclusion but for our protection. (John 17:11-16)

And **Third**, *"The Pain of Suffering."* Jesus spoke to those that were already paying the price of sacrifice and separation that real bodily pain was in their path. Not just emotional, He did that as the multitudes walked away. Not just spiritual, He did that too as His Father forsook Him while paying our sin debt. But He also experienced real physical pain. Occasionally I need a reminder that being God the Son didn't exempt Him from hunger, thirst, or real pain. He was abused and it was both brutal and painful. When He was smitten, (struck on the face) it hurt; when they yanked out His beard, it hurt; when they hit Him with rods, it hurt; when they pushed thorns into His brow, it hurt; when they scourged Him with the nine stranded whip embedded with glass, shards and steel, it hurt; and when they drove nails through His body, it hurt. Many of our forefathers in the faith were beaten, boiled, broken, burned or beheaded suffering great painful consequences of their faith. It was their persecution that ignited the spread of the gospel (good news) around the world. How is it that we feel so entitled that we should not feel pain?

In our rural church it is not uncommon to set aside an evening for "select a song" allowing folks the opportunity to request their favorite hymn to be sung. As often as she felt like she could get away with it, my mom would request hymn # 307 "Must Jesus Bare the Cross Alone", and she would always want all four verses to be sung. The opening line and title question is immediately answered, "No! There's a cross for everyone and there's a cross for me." Jesus qualified discipleship saying, "If any man will come after Me, let him deny himself, and take up his cross, and follow me." Jesus would not have made a good modern-day televangelist. He did not have a health and wealth message. He would never have preached, "Your best life now."

The Merits of This Pain

As the New Testament physician and gospel writer Luke closed out his gospel account he said, "…thus it behooved Christ to suffer, and to rise from the dead the third day:." I don't use the word "behoove" very often but when I do, I am conveying the idea that there is either a benefit for doing something or a consequence if you don't. The Apostle Paul gives us a detailed account of the consequences of Christ not suffering, dying and rising again in his first letter to the Church at Corinth in chapter fifteen. My emphasis will be on the benefits of Christ' suffering. One such benefit is that He taught us how to suffer; whether it is an injustice, or pauperizing or even death, Christ mapped out the right course, giving us an example that we should follow His steps. When I graduated from high school, a former pastor of mine, Julius Carter, gave me a book entitled, "In His Steps" by Charles M. Sheldon. This book impacted my life and set me to thinking. It must have impacted others as well because it became the second leading book for sales right behind the Bible and it was responsible in part for the "What Would Jesus Do" (WWJD) movement. I am usually not a slogan kind of guy; but this one was worth adopting.

There is no comprehensive, unabridged list of the benefits of suffering for Jesus. Every occasion of suffering yields its own unique profits. This short list may open your eyes to how rich we are for our light suffering.

- Suffering helps maintain our brokenness
- Suffering demonstrates our dependence on God
- Suffering reveals integrity
- Suffering displays a higher (divine) power
- Suffering creates opportunities to minister
- Suffering empowers others to stand
- Suffering shares God's mercy

Not to overlook the benefits given to us in the sacred text of scripture. Paul told Timothy, "if we suffer, we shall also reign with Him…." (II Timothy 2:12) To the saints in Rome he said, "…joint-heirs with Christ; if so be that we suffer with Him, that we may be also glorified together." (Romans 8:17) James, who both witnessed and experienced suffering said, "Take, my brethren, the prophets, who have spoken in the name of the Lord, for an example of suffering affliction, and of patience. Behold, we count them happy which endure." (James 5:10-11)

The Marks of This Pain

Many years ago, while studying in Exodus, I became intrigued by the provisions made for a servant who had finished his six years of servitude. He was presented with a choice of either his freedom or remaining on with his master. The caveat to this choice was that if he loved his master or had taken a wife or had children and would not leave them then his master would bore a hole in his ear against a door post. I found a great message. "A Love like that is going to leave a mark." It obviously left a mark on the servant, it also left a mark on the doorpost (things), it left a mark on the judges (others) and it made a mark on the heart of the master. (See Exodus 21:1-6) Like many other messages I have preached, it had a greater impact on me than it did the congregation. That story crossed my mind again as I contemplated the marks of pain. I have owned a few cows in the past but never did make it a business nor did I find it necessary to brand them. A rancher friend of mine tried to convince me that because of the thick hide of a cow, they really didn't feel that red-hot iron singe the hair and brand the skin. I asked, why then do you squeeze them into that tight shoot to brand them? (No good answer) The cows have never told me so, but I believe marks hurt. Not that I was about to, but I can't imagine having someone repeatedly stick you with a tattoo needle. I am not laying on a bed of nails or visiting an acupuncture therapist. I am not intentionally turning my body into a pin cushion.

Knowing Christ in His pain may scar you for life, but it might also mark you for eternity. It is only an opinion, but it is mine that Jesus had marks in His body when He ascended to Heaven and this same Jesus will come again, marks and all. The Apostle Paul stated that he bore the marks of Christ in his body. (See Galatians 6:17) Either physically or figuratively Paul was a marked man, and he didn't seem to mind it. The book of Revelation plainly teaches that some Israelites will have the seal of God in their foreheads (See Revelation 7:3 & 9:4) and another group will have the name of God in their foreheads (22:4). These marks will be a badge of honor. The last known message from the Apostle Paul, written during perilous times is recorded in Second Timothy. Paul is cheering Timothy on his walk of faith and growth in the knowledge of Christ. He said, "...endure hardness as a good soldier of Jesus Christ." (II Timothy 2:3) And "endure afflictions...." You and I are not above it and experiencing His pain would cause us to love Him even more.

My prayer: Heavenly Father, thousands before me have suffered shame, sacrificed their comforts and even given their lives for the liberty that I enjoy today. I pray that You will move me out of my comfort zone and help me trade my luxury for a cross and welcome the fellowship of your sufferings, being made conformable unto your death. Help me not resent the pain, that I might enjoy the sweet communion with your son. It is in His lovely name, the name of Jesus, that I pray, Amen.

Chapter Ten
KNOWING HIM IN HIS PRAISES

Psalm 145:3 "Great is the LORD, and greatly to be praised; and His greatness is unsearchable."

Simply defined, "Praise" is the expression of or rendering of value or worth to an object or person. To call out and recognize superior position and/or to pay homage to someone or something for excellence. Merriam Webster states it as: to express a favorable judgment of / or commend. There is nothing or no-one more worthy of commendation, recognition, homage, or favorable judgment than the LORD. He is to be greatly praised. It is not a recommendation for our consideration, but a commandment as expressed in Psalm 150. Not only is it commanded, but it is comely as well. (See Psalm 147:1) One of my favorite realities about "praise" is that there is coming a day when the voices of all the redeemed will join together in praise; it will be the anthem of the cosmic conclusion, the coronation of the Christ. (See Revelation 5: 1-14) The last five Psalms begin with the same instruction: "Praise ye the LORD." I am a proud Baptist but must acknowledge that much of the stereotype about Baptist is true (i.e.) Baptist are perceived as being anemic when it comes to praise. If we do believe it, we choose not to practice it.

The word "praise" is used 248 times in the Bible and is translated from seventeen different original language words, ten from the Old Testament and seven from the New Testament. These words provide some unique nuance or variable and/or distinction to the over-all concept of praise. Some emphasize the posture, some the sound, some the object and some the illumination or glow about the experience.

Several chapters in this book embrace the knowledge of God that produces an accompanying euphoric sensation. Knowing Him in pleasure, prayer or praise has the potential for glory bumps. My Christian experience is not measured by how warm and fuzzy I feel or how high I jump; (for sure there are times I feel more saved than other times) but it is measured on the scale of the faithfulness of Christ to keep that which I have committed unto Him. (See II Timothy 1:12 & John 10:28 -29) I along with a host of other Christians relish the moments when my glory bumps squeeze tight together or when my hallelujah meter pegs out. Unfortunately, many Christians have a highly resistant trigger to praise, I prefer to have an easy squeeze trigger (just like with my guns). I put a high premium on praise because of its eternal nature. His pleasure and our prayer closet will one day lose its relevance but our praising Him will never go out of style. We will praise Him eternally. It has been said that life is a trial run for eternity; if that is true, we may as well get accustomed to praise now because we will certainly be so inclined when we are in His presence. A preacher friend of mine illustrates moments of praise with little sayings like: "that cranks my tractor" or "if that don't light your fire, your wood is wet." What I am confident of is that nothing this side of heaven feels as good as or sounds as sweet as genuine, unpretentious, whole-hearted, Spirit motivated praise. It feels good when it feels good.

The Premise of Inherent Praise

In Luke's account of the Lord's triumphant entry into Jerusalem early in the week of His passion, Luke includes at least two evidences for the inherent nature of praise. First of which is that "the whole multitude of disciples began to rejoice and praise God with a loud voice for all the mighty works that they had seen;" (Luke 19:37) and the Second is that Jesus claimed that if they had been able to choke down His praise then "...the stone would immediately cry out." (Luke 19:40) The Psalmist invites all to participate in praise to the LORD stating that it is both pleasant and comely (Psalm 147:1). The quality of "comely" speaks of beauty that is natural or without cosmetic altering. Likewise genuine praise is pleasant and natural (not fake or put-on). It is natural to praise, but we must exercise caution to direct our praise to the one and only worthy recipient of praise. It is part of the DNA of man to praise and/or worship. We bow before, salute or honor those of superior accomplishment or higher ranking. (See Revelation 5) Inherent conveys the idea of natural, untrained or uncoached which is assuredly true of praise.

> "...Christian experience is not measured by how warm and fuzzy I feel or how high I jump..."

Sporting events often parallel life in general. It may be valuable to visit a local sporting event and pay particular attention to the level or degree of celebration from the crowd. The teams are brought on to the field to the applause of their fans. Signs of support and affirmation are throughout the stadium, the band plays the rally song, the cheerleaders jump and chant, the announcer ramps up the volume; but above the 105 dB noise can be heard the shy timid mom screaming to the top of her voice, "that's my boy." Pride and celebration merge into an emotional outburst that cannot be squelched. No apologies are necessary, everyone understands; someone that they identify with has won the race, has made the play, has defeated the enemy, has come home; that is what praise feels like.

Music and song is more than a worthwhile expression of communication from the soul to God, it is the response to an overflow of and recognition of the presence of deity. If you enjoy singing as much as I do then maybe you can relate to my many occasions, being caught off guard by an overlooked attribute of God that some author captures in the lyrics of a song. I experience an outburst of joy that demonstrates through tears or even a shout. The concept of this spontaneous eruption of praise is captured in one of the greatest gospel hymns ever written. Each verse of "How Great Thou Art" makes it clear that upon considering the creative work of God, the soul bursts into song. (Then sings my soul...) It is an inherent and deeply rooted response to personally experiencing God.

The Practice of Intentional Praise

This may be the spot where I lose some readers. You may be asking yourself, how is it possible for praise to be both "inherent" and "intentional"? Aren't those two dynamics complete opposites? If inherent means you "have to" or as I like to say, "I had a case of the can't help its" then how can it also be intentional? I do believe in and participate in an on-purpose praise. I am not ashamed to admit that sometimes I shout on purpose because God deserves it; however, that is not what I am addressing in this section. The point I am raising here is that we were created to praise that is God's intent for us. God desires praise, not to feed His inflated ego but to demonstrate our brokenness and honor His lordship. Praise is a major element of God's design for man. If no praise lifts from your lips or life, then you are missing the mark and you do not know the Lord as you should. I am not passing judgment on people that don't sing, don't cry, don't shout, don't raise their hands or don't dance unto the Lord; but I don't see anywhere that God forbids it or tempers it. In fact, the Psalmist concludes let everything that hath breath praise the Lord. (See Psalm 150:6) There is little if anything that measures up to the recognition of the sweet, powerful, and thick presence of the Lord in our midst. Although He is always near, there are times that He is overwhelmingly with us. I have sensed His presence so mightily that I felt that if I did not praise Him, I might blow a gasket. I claim to be in great company, for Paul and Silas it seemed appropriate to praise Him when they sensed His presence in their prison. The Apostle John knew He was near and praised Him while exiled on Patmos. The pew warmers that sit on their hands and never participate in praise may incorrectly quote Psalm 40:3, "And He hath put a new song in my mouth, even praise unto our God: many shall see it, and fear, and shall trust in the LORD." Notice that the Psalmist said mouth not heart. Occasionally the Psalmist even sang his prayer to the LORD. You might consider trying that with Psalm 8.

The Potential for Inhabited Praise

The doctrinal precept of our Lord's omnipresence is certainly a principal taught in the Bible. The Psalmist declared it emphatically in Psalm 139: 1–24. There is no place where one can escape the presence of God; and although this is true, there are some places especially given to or conducive to His presence. For instance: the tabernacle, the temple or where two or three are gathered in His name. (See Exodus 40:34, II Chronicles 7:1 and Matthew 18:20) There is wide debate on the meaning of Psalm 22:3 and it is not my intention to enter that debate or present myself as an authority nor do I have any interest in weighing in on the debated issues. I am not the first or only person to find sweet consolation in the concept that God can be found amidst the praises of His people. "But thou art holy, O thou that inhabitest the praises of Israel." (Psalm 22:3) It doesn't seem far-fetched to me to find the LORD nestled within the praises of His people.

There are numerable benefits to unrestrained, wholehearted praise or worship. First, saved people are drawn closer together and closer to the LORD. And second, and maybe more important is that lost people are brought under conviction and possibly born again into the family of God. The Apostle John records the words of Jesus in John 12:32 "And I, if I be lifted up from the earth, will draw all men unto me." I am completely aware that the very next verse states that Jesus said that to indicate what kind of death He would die. (Lifted up on a cross) It seems entirely plausible to me that when we are praising Him, we are also lifting Him up. I am a witness of how that has drawn sinners to Him.

The very best praise I have ever rendered has fallen miserably short of what my LORD is worthy. I decided a long time ago, it may not be all it should be but, "ain't no rocks gonna do my praising." Jesus said, "Whosoever therefore shall confess me before men, him will I confess also before my Father which is in heaven. But whosoever shall deny me before men, him will I also deny before my Father which is in heaven." (Matthew 10:32-33) And then there is the admonition of the writer of Hebrew 13:15 "By Him therefore let us offer the sacrifice of praise to God continually, that is, the fruit of our lips giving thanks to His name." The apostle Paul stated that he was not ashamed of the gospel. Neither was he ashamed to praise or worship his Lord. If I must ere between too little or too much praise, I choose to go all in. I have been in services where blood bought believers sit so reverently that they resemble the stadium poster people from the pandemic days. When Jesus passed through Samaria, He provided insight to acceptable worship. It must be done in Spirit and in truth. (See John 4: 23-24) If you have the joy, joy, joy, joy down in your heart; it might be time to let it out.

My Prayer: "Heavenly Father, I confess that my praise is woefully weak and fails to reveal the joy that You have placed within me. If the world was depending on my praise to point them to You then I have failed them and You alike. Father, I want to know You so intimately that Your praises flow freely from my lips. Please forgive me for sitting on my hands and zipping my lips when it was time to shout. In Jesus name I pray. Amen

Chapter Eleven
Knowing Him in Prayer

I Kings 8:54–56 & 60 "And it was so, that when Solomon had made an end of praying all this prayer and supplication unto the LORD, he arose from before the altar of the LORD, from kneeling on his knees with his hands spread up to heaven. And he stood, and blessed all the congregation of Israel with a loud voice, saying, Blessed be the LORD, that hath given rest unto His people Israel… That all the people of the earth may know that the LORD is God, and that there is none else."

In the pursuit of "Knowing Him", many approaches or methods might be used to discover insights into who The LORD really is. One of the most intimate types of knowledge that a person can obtain is gained through one-on-one close encounters. It is not impossible to know someone casually through group contact or team experience, but true colors are discovered under the bright light of private scrutiny and repeated contact under extreme conditions. The God of Heaven has afforded us the blessed opportunity to approach into His divine presence under any and all circumstances for an exclusive private meeting. We can ask anything we want to without worry of ridicule or embarrassment. We use terms like let down your guard, let your hair down, or come clean to describe the moments when we share the most intimate information. We often shy away from revealing the kinks in our armor as if no one can see them unless we point them out, but the friends or family or work associates that spend copious hours at our side know all too well the flaws and our shortcomings. God certainly knows all about us and is not caught off guard with our confessions. Conversely, that intimate time with God will reveal no inadequacies or flaws to His character or actions and will assist us in the pursuit that we claim to crave. Instead, what we find is a treasure chest full of flawless and priceless gemstones. The opportunity to know the LORD through prayer has been granted to us without restriction and in fact we are not only encouraged to pray but commanded to pray. If anyone claims to really know the LORD and doesn't talk with Him regularly, he is dishonest or deceived. To know Him creates an insatiable appetite to communicate with Him regularly and more frequently, much like an addiction demands more and more.

The Elements of Prayer

The complex components of prayer may shed light on what it takes to grow in your knowledge of the LORD through or during your prayer life. Prayer is so profound that it reaches the spectrum of simple and complex at the same time. There is very little as precious as the prayer of an innocent young child that hasn't learned any different than to completely trust that God is always listening and that He can do anything. They don't know all the protocols or rules, they haven't learned a profound prayer language. They just climb up on God's lap and smile, love and ask. It is also beautiful when we read or recite the poetic prayers of Israel's psalmist or eavesdrop on the prayer of an aged saint. God looks forward to unpretentious conversations with His children. Nevertheless, there are some considerations available that might make God more visible or personal as we pray.

Let us look first at **The Place of Prayer.** This is not to suggest that there is a wrong place to pray. Absolutely not, the Apostle Paul told young Timothy that he wished "...that men pray every where...." (See I Timothy 2:8) There are some places specifically mentioned in the Bible where prayer seems to have been successfully offered. Jesus "...went up into a **mountain** apart to pray..." Matthew 14:23. Jesus also prayed while in a **garden** and while at the **table** in the upper room and lest we forget He also prayed from the **cross**. Jonah prayed from the **belly of a whale**, Paul and Silas prayed from **prison**, Stephen from his **stoning pit** and Daniel prayed from his **window** toward Jerusalem. The Temple of the Old Testament and the Church of the New Testament are to be known as the House of Prayer. All these sites are wonderful places to pray and no doubt they are places to grow in knowledge of the LORD. I am particularly fond of Luke's account of when the Lord's disciples asked Him to teach them to pray. Luke records that the Lord was "praying in a **certain place**." (See Luke 11:1) If there is a more productive place to pray than some other place then it behooves us to find that place. In Matthew 6:6 Jesus taught His disciples to enter into their closet, close the door, and pray in secret. I have looked at hundreds of house-plans and am yet to see a house with a dedicated room for prayer, like a closet or perhaps a war room. The most lethal yet neglected weapon in the Christian arsenal is prayer; we sing about the "Sweet Hour of Prayer" and are content to squeeze it into forty-five seconds. Corporate prayer is wonderful, (i.e.) where we all agree in prayer, and one leads in prayer. Communal prayer is fine, (i.e.) where multiple people pray simultaneously. But closet prayer is where we get to know Him best. To my shame, in times of corporate prayer I find myself weighing the theology of the prayer or the words or repetition rather than praying for myself in silent agreement to the public prayer. In times of communal praying, I am not focused enough to keep from being distracted. Some folks can watch TV, do the dishes, and finish their homework at the same time and never miss a beat with any of those tasks. I am not that guy. I agree with a song writer from years ago that penned the words to "All Alone." He stated that Jesus is the pattern for us all, All Alone. If we'll only steel away in some portion of the day we will find it always pays to be alone.

> *"The most lethal yet neglected weapon in the Christian arsenal is prayer..."*

Another element of prayer is **The Posture of Prayer.** There is a similarity of thought between the place of prayer and the posture of prayer in that there is no wrong posture for praying like there is no wrong place. If you find yourself in a foxhole fighting for your life, then bunkered down beneath your helmet is a great posture. Solomon **knelt down** with his hands raised toward heaven. **Prostrate** appears to be an often-used position. In Nehemiah chapter nine the children of Israel stood and confessed their sins and the Levites **stood** and cried out to the LORD their God. The clear conclusion is that it is the posture of the heart and not the body that matters. A person with a contrite / broken heart can approach God from a dusty road with sackcloth and ashes or from a throne with a crown of gold on their head. It is the posture of the heart that makes the difference to the LORD. Because of Christ we may come boldly (not arrogantly) to the throne of God. Confident that God hears us and if He hears us, He will answer us according to His will. Jesus is **seated** at the right-hand of the Father making intercession for us. If our heart is right, He will hear us.

A third element of prayer is **The Purpose of Prayer.** What motivates your prayer is of utmost importance to God. James records in his epistle, "Ye ask, and receive not, because ye ask amiss, that ye may consume it upon your lusts." (James 4:3) James addresses what is a wrong motive or purpose and of necessity acknowledges that there must be a right motive or purpose. Just a few paragraphs back I bragged on the young child that did not know any trade secrets to prayer and yet touched the heart of God with their simplicity. That child embraces several of the purposes of prayer. Clearly portrayed is the concept of <u>communion with God</u>. The famous hymnist, Dottie Rambo, wrote a brilliant song on this subject entitled, "I Just Came To Talk With You Lord." The idea that someone can come and not ask for anything reveals a pure motive; just wanting to spend time with or getting to know the LORD. There is so much more that the LORD wants to reveal of Himself if we would just give Him the time. There is no reward for speed when it comes to prayer, God is not in a hurry. Also included in the child's prayer is <u>requests</u>; it is not wrong or impolite to ask God. He said, "Ask, and it shall be given you..." (Matthew 7:7). Contrary to many Televangelists, this is not a genie in a bottle kind of verse but rather an introduction to a Jehovah Jireh kind of God that will provide for His children. God wants to be proven and He will always be found faithful. James 4:2 reads, "Ye lust, and have not: ye kill, and desire to have, and cannot obtain: ye fight and war, yet ye have not, because ye ask not." If we who are evil give good things to our children, how much more does God give good things to His children. (See Luke 11:9-13) In these last days a generation of unthankful people stand expecting a hand-out as if they are entitled to what everybody else has. Paul warned Timothy that in the last days we would face perilous times, he said, "For men shall be lovers of their own selves, covetous, boasters, proud, blasphemers, disobedient to parents, unthankful, unholy," (II Timothy 3:2). The unthankful element of the last days has spilled over into our prayer lives. God enjoys receiving thanks from His children and thanksgiving should be routine in our prayers. When writing to the Church in Philippi, Paul instructed them to "Be careful for nothing; but in every thing by prayer and supplication with thanksgiving let your requests be made known unto God." (Philippians 4:6) High up in the list of purposes for prayer is intercession. Many examples of intercessory prayer can be found in the Bible and beyond examples there is the command to pray for others. Listen to Paul's exhortation to Timothy on this subject, "I exhort therefore, that, first of all, supplications, prayers, intercessions, and giving of thanks, be made for all men;."

The last element of prayer that I will discuss is **The Persistence of Prayer**. Being persistent in prayer does not suggest the lack of faith. Faith and persistence are not in competition or mutually exclusive. Jesus prayed three times for the cup to pass. Paul prayed three times for the thorn to be removed. This does not constitute "vain repetition" (See Matthew 6:7) but demonstrates the severity of our request or the depths of our sorrow. David prayed in the evening, in the morning and at noon. (See Psalm 55:17) We are told to pray without ceasing (See I Thessalonians 5:17 and Romans 12:12) On two occasions Jesus emphasized the value of persistence or importunity. The first is found in Luke 11:5-8 and immediately follows the Lord teaching His disciples to pray and involves a man persistently asking his friend for bread late in the night. The friend gets up from bed and gives him the bread. The second account is found in Luke 18: 1-8 and deals with a widow troubling a judge for vindication and by her persistence the judge does avenge her of her adversary. The Lord commends both of these persistent people. The lesson is not that the LORD must be beat down by our perpetual annoying request before He will grant us what we desire; but that there is persuasive value in our repetitive asking.

The Efficacy of Prayer

This area of study maximizes the accomplishments that result from very intense prayer. This is not a blanket coverage of everything that is called prayer. Unfortunately, Christians get caught up in memorized verbiage that sounds both sanctimonious and soothing but lacks the sincerity to clear the ceiling. If we want the audience of God and the fruition of our desires, then it demands that we follow the guidebook and methodology established by the One who answers. Jesus said, "And whatsoever ye shall ask in my name, that will I do, that the Father may be glorified in the Son. If ye shall ask any thing in my name, I will do it." (John 14:13-14) (See also John 16:23) Mark provides us with the detail of the importance of <u>believing</u> in Mark 11:24. Similarly James mentions the prayer of <u>faith</u> in James 5:15. The evidence is that without faith, you are only offering up religious monologue and wasting your time. In the subsequent verse James qualifies the kind of prayers that avail much (i.e.) effectual <u>fervent</u>. Those back-to-back words suggest successful passionately intense praying will get results from God.

Successful prayers are directed to the Father (as Jesus taught His disciples to pray) and they are assisted by the aid of the Spirit which helps our infirmities. Romans 8:26 reads, "Likewise the Spirit also helpeth our infirmities: for we know not what we should pray for as we ought: but the Spirit itself maketh intercession for us with groanings which cannot be uttered." They are presented to the Father by our advocate and only mediator Jesus Christ (See I Timothy 2:5) and as our mediator He has a fiduciary responsibility to advocate in our behalf. Our heavenly Father knows the things that we need before we ask, but He is pleased to hear our prayer and attend to our cry, it is our admission of dependency. In all our praying it is critical that we yield our own will to His. Jesus in the prayer classroom taught His disciples to pray "...Thy will be done in earth, as it is in heaven." (Matthew 6:10) It is also clearly taught in the inspired writing of the Apostle John. He wrote in I John 5:14-15 "And this is the confidence that we have in Him, that, if we ask any thing <u>according to His will</u>, He heareth us: And if we know that He hear us, whatsoever we ask, we know that we have the petitions that we desired of Him."

This chapter is not just learning how to pray but learning to pray and wait on Him. We will get to know Him as we commune with Him. It is no accident that "close" and "closet" are so similar. Many years ago, my brother-in-law was called and accepted the pastorate of a small rural church in Georgia. After years of faithful service to them, the church experienced uncommon growth. They were ministering to thousands of members at three different morning services each week. This phenomenon caught the attention of pastors everywhere which flocked to his office and campus to discover the secret of success. After repeatedly crediting God with the success and naming prayer as the ingredient most responsible, his admirers were not content. They often said, "we believe in prayer" to which he eventually responded everybody believes in it, we practice it.

My prayer: "My heavenly Father, I bow my head and acknowledge my woefully inadequate prayer life. I have expected you to wait in the closet for my untimely arrival and even then, I hurry through my wish list with no thought of the high honor bestowed on me. One that allows me into the halls of heaven. You have given me access to the wealth of heaven and the opportunity to rest in your presence, to hear your heartbeat, to feel your embrace, and to experience uninterrupted love. Please forgive me for my neglect and the selfish motives that drive me to my knees. Let me experience your glory and simply to find joy in your presence. I am not worthy of the manifold blessings that have come to me, but I thank you and pray in the name of your Son, Jesus Christ, amen.

Chapter Twelve
KNOWING HIM IN HIS PROMISES

I Kings 8:56 "Blessed be the LORD, that hath given rest unto His people Israel, according to all that He promised: there hath not failed one word of all His good promise, which He promised by the hand of Moses His servant."

I have previously shared the importance of music and song in my life. I find a song for every situation, or I write one if I cannot find one. Sixty years ago, I learned a children's song that claimed, "Every promise in the Book is mine, every chapter every verse every line, all the blessings of His love divine, every promise in the Book is mine." Although theologically that may not be accurate, practically it is because even if I am not the primary audience of a promise, every promise kept lends credibility to the viability that the balance of promises eventually will be kept.

There are many words used or methods of conveying a promise. The word "promise" or some variation of it is used 115 times in the Bible. Many other words that offer the same guarantee are likewise used. For instance, vow (est, ed, s) totals 91 occasions, covenant(s) 295 times, will or shall over 13,000 times. Once the LORD said His name would be at stake if His promise failed to materialize (See Isaiah 55:13). A Canadian school teacher, Everett R. Storms, went on a mission to discover the correct number of promises in the Bible. His conclusion was that there are 8,810 promises recorded in Scripture and 7,487 of those are from God to mankind.

We are prone to trivialize promises. We make them and break them without so much as a regret. Our signature on a promissory note, our vows at a wedding or making cheap promises while amidst punishment; "I promise I will never do it again" demonstrate our shallow opinion of promises. Sometimes our promises are bargaining chips in trade for God to heal our loved one or to bail us out of self-inflicted storms. "Lord if you will ... then I will be in church every Sunday for the rest of my life." Sometimes our intentions are great, and we genuinely plan and purpose to fulfill our promises but then sometimes we know better than that when we make them, these are often referred to as political promises. God is not frivolous concerning promises, neither His nor ours. Not only is He completely capable of keeping His promise, but He is also faithful to honor His promise, in His own time and way. The Apostle Peter reminds us of this faithfulness in II Peter 3:9 "The Lord is not slack concerning His promise, as some men count slackness; but is longsuffering to us-ward, not willing that any should perish, but that all should come to repentance." God's Word contains a wide variety of promises made from God to man. Many have been fulfilled others will be soon. Among the promises from God, you can find: the promised seed, the promised land, promised increase, promised people, promised rest, promised victory, promised wisdom, promised reign, promised goodness, promised light, promised eternal life, promised shaking of heaven and earth, promised crown, promised kingdom, promised resurrection and a promised return; just to name a few.

Many folks claim that there are only two things that you can be sure of death and taxes. And while you may be sure of those, I must add one more; God's word is sure. In fact, Peter shared that truth in his second epistle "We have also a more sure word of prophecy; whereunto ye do well that ye take heed, as unto a light that shineth in a dark place, until the day dawn, and the day star arise in your hearts:" (II Peter 1:19) If God said it, that settles it. Paul the apostle spoke of sure promises in Romans chapter four and verse sixteen while encouraging saints concerning faith and grace. God's promises are sure not only based upon His faithfulness but His perfect knowledge of the end from the beginning. Nothing will surprise Him or derail His promises.

The Person of the Promise

God is not man and will never make promises with His fingers crossed. While well intentioned men may break a promise, that is not true of God. At least three places in Scripture assert that God's word is absolute and reliable. Notice first in Numbers 23:19 what Moses pinned before his death, "God is not a man, that He should lie; neither the son of man, that He should repent: hath He said, and shall He not do it? Or hath He spoken, and shall He not make it good?." Moses had met the Lord and knew Him as well as any man ever has. His experience with the LORD was that He keeps His word. A passage in Hebrews 6:18 states, "...it was impossible for God to lie..." and in Hebrews 10:23 we find, "...(for He is faithful that promised;)." One other great text on the subject is found in Titus 1:2 which reads, "In hope of eternal life which God, that cannot lie, promised before the world began;." If the word of the Lord could somehow be stopped or thwarted, then He would not or could not be God. It would pollute His character, mar His image, and stain His pure garment. The Bible declares that His ways are not only different than our ways but higher than our ways. (See Isaiah 55:9) The integrity of the Word of God (Bible) hinges on the reliability of the promises of God. How can a God be trusted who does not faithfully honor His word. An attorney is very careful to not put on the stand an unreliable witness or one whose credibility has been compromised. God has not nor will He ever fail. Because He is God, "I am standing on the promises that cannot fail, when the howling storms of doubt and fear assail, by the living word of God I shall prevail, Standing on the Promises of God."

The Power of the Promise

I can promise things like: the sun will come up in the morning, there will never be another universal flood, there will be "...seedtime and harvest, and cold and heat, and summer and winter, and day and night..." so long as the earth remains, (Genesis 8:22) because it does not depend upon my ability to keep those promises. All I am doing is piggy-backing on the promises of God who has all power to make it happen. A promise is only as good as the ability or strength of the one who makes the promise. When General MacArthur promised the allied forces on Corregidor that he would return, there was great reason to question whether he would be able to keep the promise; namely, the strength of the Imperial Japanese Army that stood in his way. God too has His enemies, but they are no match for His infinite power. His enemies could never intercept His promises.

> *"If the word of the Lord could somehow be stopped or thwarted, then He would not or could not be God."*

God has made some outlandish or bizarre promises that could never be kept by mere mortal. For instance, "I will never leave thee, nor forsake thee." The writer of Hebrews (13:5) quoted from Deuteronomy 31:6 where Moses encouraged the nation of Israel that God would always be with them especially during the tough times of claiming their promised land. Paul offered that same encouragement to the saints at Rome in Romans 4:21 "And being fully persuaded that, what He had promised, He was able also to perform." On the occasions of driving through to visit my bank teller once I have placed my tube into the vacuum, I spend the waiting moments reading the notice on the machine, that my deposit is guaranteed by the FDIC with the full strength of the United States Department of the Treasury. You cannot imagine how comforting and reassuring that is to me.

The Purpose of the Promise

Mankind has demonstrated the possession of an ego that must be pampered. We make promises to impress or to persuade. God has a far greater motivation behind His promises. With each of His promises His motive is revealed,

He promises to be with us, to provide for us, to love us, to care for us, and to return for us; all to relieve us of the burdens of life. Jesus said, "take no thought..." concerning the needs of life, "...for your heavenly Father knoweth that ye have need of these things. But seek ye first the kingdom of God, and His righteousness; and all these things shall be added unto you." (Matthew 6:25-33)

There are at least two Biblical reasons for God making and recording His promises to us: <u>Purity</u> and <u>Partaking</u>. In II Corinthians 7:1 Paul records, "Having therefore these promises, dearly beloved, let us cleanse ourselves from all filthiness of the flesh and spirit, perfecting holiness in the fear of God." While this verse details the purpose of **purity** that is behind the promise, we need to back up to the preceding chapter to find out the nature of the promise. Chapter six concludes with the if/then promise that if we come out from among them and are separate and touch not the unclean thing then the Lord will receive us and be to us a Father. (See II Corinthians 6:17-18) The Apostle Paul considered that to be such a bargain that no one in their right mind would dare miss out on the chance. He said, "let us" indicating that he was signed on to it and expected those at Corinth to sign on also. God's refining work to reflect Himself in us is the backdrop to all His precious promises.

The second purpose behind God's promise is found in II Peter 1:4, where Peter, who had heard the Lord's promises made and kept, said, "Whereby are given unto us exceeding great and precious promises: that by these ye might be **partakers** of the divine nature, having escaped the corruption that is in the world through lust." God's promises are intended to develop in us Christlikeness; that the divine nature might overtake the carnal one and allow us to escape or avoid the corruption that plagues the world around us. That lust will not overpower us. With a promise of victory ahead and all provisions necessary for the journey why should we fret. Over 130 years ago, the great song writer, Russell K. Carter, wrote and put to music the classic hymn "Standing on the

Promises." That song gives attention to the fact that we overcome daily through the Spirit's sword and that we rest in our Savior as our all in all.

I began this journey of "Knowing Him" with you many pages ago and proclaimed that I had not arrived at my destination. I am however more committed than ever to continue with fervor my pursuit of Him. One day I will know Him even as He is known, when I see Him face to face. But until then the journey continues...

My prayer: Heavenly Father, the desire of my heart is to know you, and to passionately seek that knowledge and your favor, to wholeheartedly serve you, to worship you, to share you, to enjoy you and be found faithful until you fulfill your promise and come to take me to be ever with you. May my life cause others to have a desire to know and pursue you. You alone are worthy of such devotion. Please forgive my fickle focus and allow me to draw close to you, that I might behold your glory like never before. I am and forever shall be yours. In Jesus lovely name I pray, Amen.

BAPTIST TRAINING CENTER PUBLICATIONS
WINTER HAVEN, FLORIDA

Made in the USA
Columbia, SC
26 January 2023